Franklin R. Elliott, Francis C. Maroni

Popular Deciduous and Evergreen Trees and Shrubs

for planting in parks, gardens, cemeteries, etc.

Franklin R. Elliott, Francis C. Maroni

Popular Deciduous and Evergreen Trees and Shrubs
for planting in parks, gardens, cemeteries, etc.

ISBN/EAN: 9783337335403

Printed in Europe, USA, Canada, Australia, Japan

Cover: Foto ©Andreas Hilbeck / pixelio.de

More available books at **www.hansebooks.com**

POPULAR

Deciduous and Evergreen

TREES AND SHRUBS,

FOR PLANTING IN

PARKS, GARDENS, CEMETERIES, ETC., ETC.

BY

F. R. ELLIOTT,

Landscape Gardener and Pomologist,

AUTHOR OF "WESTERN FRUIT BOOK," ETC.

———— ❖ ————

NEW YORK:

GEO. E. WOODWARD, 191 BROADWAY.

1870.

PREFACE.

THE preparation of the following pages has not been with intention to exhibit or inculcate anything specially new, but rather to put in plain, every-day accessible form some features connected with trees and shrubs for planting in streets, parks, private grounds, cemeteries, etc., and their value for such purposes, that would readily enable the improver of a new place to answer for himself a question often asked, viz., "What shall I plant?"

I have endeavored, in plain language, to depict the leading prominent habits of trees, to give somewhat of the heights, etc., to which they attain, and the soils in which they best succeed. I have also ventured to suggest some of the places and positions in which their use will be most satisfactory.

I have made no attempt to give a list of all known trees and shrubs, nor to classify them scientifically; nor yet have I designed to forestall the needs of a landscape gardener in the creation of taste and effect; but have written with a view to meet a popular and general want of the public when performing their own planting, as brought to my knowledge in my professional life.

If the hints here offered assist, even to a limited extent, in creating more judicious placing of tree or shrub in private gardens or public cemeteries, the object of writing will be accomplished; and with hope thereof it is offered to the public.

CLEVELAND, OHIO, *June*, 1868.

AGRICULTURAL BOOKS.

FOR SALE BY

GEO. E. WOODWARD,

191 BROADWAY,

NEW YORK.

☞ *Any Book on this List will be forwarded, post-paid, to any address in the United States or Territories, on receipt of the price.*

NEW PUBLICATIONS :

American Cattle. By L. F. Allen. $2.50
Downing's Fruits and Fruit Trees of America. Revised and greatly enlarged. Octavo. 1122 pp..$7.50
Agricultural Chemical Analysis.................$2.00
    By Prof. G. C. Caldwell of Cornell University.
Practical Poultry Keeper. By L. Wright.... $2.00
Parsons on the Rose. By Samuel B. Parsons.........$1.50
Practical Floriculture. By P. Henderson............$1.50
New American Farm Book. By L. F. Allen.......$2.50
Farm Impl'ts and Machinery. By J. J. Thomas..$1.50
Market Assistant. By Thomas F. De Voe............$2.50
Hunter and Trapper. By an Old Hunter....... $1.00
Gardening for the South. By W. N. White........$2.00
Tim Bunker Papers...... ....$1.50
How Crops Grow. By Prof. S. W. Johnson..........$2.00
How Crops Feed. By Prof. S. W. Johnson............$2.00
The Percheron Horse...................................$1.00
Darwin's Variation of Animals and Plants Under Domestication, 2 Volumes.................$6.00
The Book of Evergreens. By J. Hoopes............$3.00
Cotton Culture. By J. B. Lyman. $1.50
Draining for Profit and Health. By Waring.....$1.50
The Grape Vine. By Prof. Frederick Mohr..........$1.00
American Pomology. By Dr. J. A. Warder..........$3.00
Small Fruit Culturist. By A. S. Fuller........... $1.50
Gardening for Profit. By P. Henderson.............$1.50
SPECIAL.
Harney's Barns, Out-buildings, & Fences..$10.00
Woodward's National Architect........ ....$12.00

CONTENTS.

POPULAR
DECIDUOUS AND EVERGREEN
TREES AND SHRUBS.

CHAPTER I.

INTRODUCTORY.

"A TASTE for rural improvements of every description," says Downing, "is advancing silently, but with great rapidity in this country." This is evident from the immense number of trees and shrubs that are planted from year to year in all private and public grounds, upon the borders of our country roads, the streets of our small towns and villages, and the suburbs of large cities.

As a nation we progress rapidly in the accumulation of wealth, and perhaps we may with safety be called a "money-getting people;" but with all our love of money it has thus far in the course been gained more for the enjoyments it would purchase, or the good the owner was enabled to do therewith, than for the simple, yet base, purpose of hoarding. While we have no law to compel a man to plant a tree upon the roadside on reaching manhood's age, or upon the birth of each child, we have as a people so much of enterprise and taste, so much ambition and love of home adornment, that we are unwilling to rest quiet without the association, comfort, and enjoyment in all ways derived from cooling shades and fragrant flowers.

We are yet a young people, and in many places the trees that adorn our homes and our streets have grown with our growth; and while we are to pass away, they are to remain life-enduring monuments of our labors and examples of instruction to our children's children for generations to come.

In years gone by, our street shades, as well as those adorning our homes, had to contend against depredations of roving cattle, horses, etc.; but thanks to the courts, and more recently to some of our State laws, it is fast coming to the comprehension of the multitude, that our roadways are public property only as they may be properly and soberly used as passage-ways, and that otherwise they belong to the owners of the land adjoining. When this feature is more generally known and adopted, we look to see our roadways and public pleasure drives more generally adorned with tree and shrub in front of each man's land as may please his taste or suit the position.

More variety of trees can also be safely planted; and as the light wire fences or well-trimmed hedges gradually take the place of heavy boards, rails, or pickets, our roadways will soon present more the appearance of park drives than pathways to market.

In the following pages it has been the object of the author to so plainly describe each tree and shrub, with its adaptation to positions and soils, that the most complete novice in tree planting may read and understand, and thereby advance the beauty of our roadsides, cemeteries, and private homes.

CHAPTER II.

DECIDUOUS TREES.

THE ASH—*Fraxinus.*—There are many varieties of the ash, all more or less valuable both as ornamental shade trees and for timber uses. The European ash—*fraxinus excelsior*—is a lofty tree, with more of a spreading head than our American—*fraxinus Americanus*—varieties, and is the one generally grown and sold at the nurseries. As a street tree, along suburban or country roads, and for creating apparent elevations in landscape, or for forming the point tree of a background, both the European and American are good. We prefer the European for street planting, and the American for effect in the landscape, but use it only in grounds of considerable extent.

For places of small extent, both the European and American are of too large growth. A rich, deep, and moist, almost wet, soil suits the ash best; but it succeeds well in almost any soil or situation, being very hardy and entirely free from insects.

Of the fancy varieties, the GOLD-BARKED (*aurea*) is most notable, because of the bright yellow of its branches, forming with its singular contorted or irregular, upright, spreading growth a conspicuous object in winter. The WILLOW-LEAVED (*salicifolia*) has narrow wavy leaves, and is perhaps one of the strongest growers; while the MYRTLE-LEAVED (*viridis*) is of a stunted or dwarfed habit with very dark green myrtle-like leaves, and is valuable only as a curiosity, or for a position on the point of two diverging roads or paths; and for this latter purpose perhaps a better variety is one under the name of DWARF GLOBE-HEADED, which originated with Messrs. Ellwanger

1*

& Barry, of Rochester, N. Y.; this, when grafted or budded on stocks of the *excelsior* or *Americana*, at a height of about six feet, forms a very pleasing ornamental dwarf tree.

Of the other varieties, such as the crisp-leaved, gold blotched-leaved, etc., we have no occasion here to speak, because they are only desirable in very large collections, where variety rather than beauty or usefulness is the object sought.

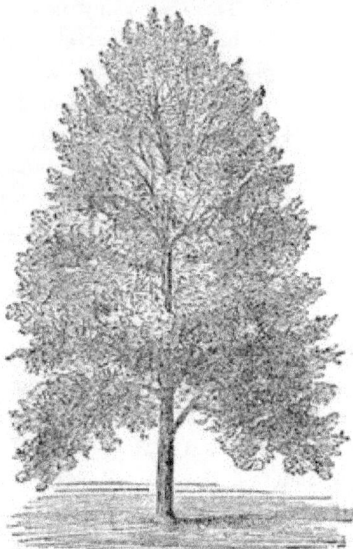

FIG. 1.—AMERICAN ASH.

The FLOWERING ASH—*ornus Europæus*—is a tree of an entire different habit. While an ash, and growing rapidly when young, it soon appears to have become mature, and seldom gets above twenty to thirty feet high, with a round ball-like head of about fifteen to twenty feet diameter. Its clean foliage and regular habit, together with the numerous white flowers which it bears in May or June, according to the climate in which it is grown, renders it desirable for planting in grounds of an extent of two or more acres. There is a variety of this, *macrophylla*, with larger foliage and stronger growth, that is desirable where two or more trees are to be planted.

AILANTUS—*Glandulosa*.—The Chinese Ailantus, or Tree of Heaven as it is often called, has received much fulsome praise and equally unjust censure. It is a tree that grows rapidly, and in almost any soil; is entirely free from insects, and although not graceful, yet its strong shoots or arms of rusty brown young wood, taken with its long and singular foliage and profusion of whitish green flowers, create a tree of no mean attraction. There are two sexes, both of which produce flowers, the male much less abundantly than the female; and while the male suckers freely, the female does not. It should never be planted near dwellings, or where the ground is to be dug. It grows freely while young; but once it has attained a height of fifteen to twenty feet and comes into flowering, it increases in size more slowly.

BEECH—*Fagus*.—Our AMERICAN BEECH—*fagus Americana*—we rank as combining in itself more of beauty, grace, and magnificence than perhaps any other of our forest trees. True, it has not the grandeur of the oak; but with its stateliness of upright, spreading growth, every line and twig is one of graceful ease; and from the first opening of the buds in spring, onward until in full foliage, its glossiness and changing shades are a constant and varying feature of beauty. In winter, its delicate spray combined with the prominence of its long pointed buds make it especially an object of attraction and admiration. Some planters object to the beech on account of a tendency to sucker, but we have never found it so where the roots remained unbroken by cultivation.

Young trees should always be procured with branches starting from near the ground, and rarely does it need the knife applied to give it regularity and symmetry of form. A deep loamy, rather moist soil gives it most vigor and causes it to grow to a large size; but it also grows freely in poor thin soils, as the roots spread widely and keep near the surface. It is admirably adapted to grouping with the hemlock, and with *sequoia gigantea*, or the mammoth evergreen tree of California; but as a single lawn tree it has no superior, and should be planted wherever

FIG. 2.—AMERICAN BEECH.

room can be given for its development without destroying breadth or character of grounds.

Of fancy varieties of the beech, the true purple-leaved (*purpurea*) is the most desirable. It has rather stronger limbs and twigs than the common plain variety, and the young shoots and buds are of a rose color, while the foliage when young or half grown is of a reddish purple tinge, forming a pleasing and attractive contrast with the green of other trees. The cut-leaved (*incisa*) forms, while young, a vigorous, well-marked tree with leaves variously cut, resembling in some cases ferns, in others willows; as it gets age, however, these markings of the foliage become less and less distinct. The crested, silver, and gold-striped leaved varieties are all singular and pretty, but their growth is feeble, rendering them only desirable for an arboretum. The oak-leaved (*quercifolia*) and large-leaved (*macrophylla*) are varieties of comparatively new introduction, and may prove valuable for general planting, but as yet it can only be advisable to give them place in large grounds.

BIRCH—*Betula.*—Few of our native trees grow more rapidly while young, or are more easily transplanted than the birch. It grows freely in any soil, not wet; and where a graceful, light-foliaged tree is wanted, few have better claims on the planter's attention. There are many varieties, some of them growing only a few feet high, as *fruticosa, nana,* etc.; but the common black birch (*nigra*), and the tall birch (*excelsa*), together with the European white birch (*alba*), are the varieties most in use. They are admirable for crowning a rocky point or ledge; for grouping with the larch or hemlock, and by their pensile spray and adaptation to poor soils well suited for planting in cemeteries. In autumn, the foliage when about to drop off becomes a bright yellow or scarlet.

BUTTERNUT—*Juglans cinerea.*—Although not strictly to be classed among ornamental trees, yet the rapidity of growth while young, the habit of early bearing, together with the great value of its fruit, make the butternut a tree desirable to plant wherever a suitable place can be found. Its branches spread out horizontally, so that often the tree has more breadth than height, and its foliage is so sparse that it must not be counted upon as a shade under which to rest from the noonday sun; but if there is a rich spot of ground—for it requires rich soil—where this tree can be grown, our advice is to plant it. It groups well with the Austrian or Scotch pines.

CATALPA—*Syringafolia.*—A native of our Southern States, the catalpa or shavanon is one of our most showy as well as rapid growing trees. Unfortunately it is not quite hardy in our Northern sections, and can not safely be introduced and planted except in positions where it can have some protection from our bright suns of winter. It is a tree that is suitable for

FIG. 3.—BUTTERNUT.

grouping with the Austrian, Scotch ,or yellow pines; but when grown singly, its masses of white and purple flowers render it a tree of beauty unequaled only by the Paulownia. As a street or park tree, wherever it will endure the winters, it is one of the best. A light dry soil is best suited to its growth.

CHESTNUT—*Castanea.*—The perfect hardihood, rapid growth, erect yet spreading head, clean glossy foliage, entirely exempt from insects, and the richness of its fruit render our common sweet chestnut more worthy of attention and liberal planting than it has ever received.

As a park or street tree, its very habit of yielding good fruit we suppose would be the first objection made to its introduction, because of the liability of its branches being broken by reckless boys and lawless men. We can only say this is no fault of the tree, but is a bad mark for those who educate the boys, and an indication that we have many laws that are made only to be broken.

Every planter of private grounds who has room should use the chestnut, as it is in itself as a tree beautiful, whether singly or in groups, of easy cultivation, and produces fruit of value as profitable one year with another as an apple-tree. A light, dry, yet rich soil suits it best, but it will grow in any good soil that is well drained. It is somewhat difficult to transplant after the trees are more than three years from the seed, but by cutting around the roots one season previous, trees of considerable size can be safely removed.

The French Marron or Spanish chestnut we have found equally hardy, and as their fruit is much larger where the trees can be had, they will be the best.

COFFEE TREE— *Gymnocladus.* —The Kentucky coffee tree (*gymnocladus canadensis*) is a singular tree, remarkable and always attracting attention, but without any feature that would otherwise call it into use as one to plant in ornamenting grounds. Its wood has no appearance of buds, and in winter it looks like a dead tree; but when it puts on its foliage, which is often very long and wide, and of a dull bluish green, its character is very much improved. As a curiosity in large collections it is desirable. Rich, deep, moist soil gives it the greatest vigor.

CHERRY—*Cerasus.*—Under the name of wild or BIRD CHERRY there are several varieties popularly recognized, but only that classed by botanists as *Virginiana* is desirable for parks or private grounds. The tree grows rapidly, and while its slender branches droop, its form is upright, spreading, and when in good soil attaining a very large size. Like the birch, graceful and pliant, swaying to every breeze its glossy foliage in the summer season; and its delicate, long, slender, purplish red spray in winter make the bird cherry a very desirable tree for many situations.

As a street tree it would be unsuitable, and for small grounds it grows too large. Birds seem attracted always to it, and nest in it perhaps more than in any other tree.

The PERFUMED or MAHALEB CHERRY is another variety of great beauty and value as an ornamental tree. It makes a small or dwarf tree of only fifteen to twenty feet high, and may be grown in any soil, from the very poorest to its opposite. For planting in cemeteries and small private grounds, its light and abundant spray, pale green leaves, strong yet agreeable perfume of wood, flowers, and fruit, make for it a strong claim for position. As a foreground also to groups of larger growing trees, whether evergreen or deciduous, it is admirable.

The DOUBLE FLOWERING CHERRY, a variety of the heart cherries, from its vigorous growth and profusion of double white flowers, like miniature roses in early spring, is a valuable tree for roadsides in the country, inclosed parks, or extensive private grounds.

DECIDUOUS CYPRESS—*Taxodium distichia.*—Although a native of our Southern States, the deciduous cypress proves hardy in our Middle and also over a great portion of our Northern States. In foliage it is different from all other trees; with a resemblance to the hemlock, it has a light bright green leaf combined with an airy lightness of great elegance, pleasing and attractive to all. In low, wet grounds, as in its native habitat, it grows to a large tree; but planted in our common garden soils, it forms a tree of only medium height, say

twenty to thirty feet. As it pushes its roots deep into the
ground, it is always best to transplant young trees. In private
grounds of an acre or more extent, one or more trees should
always be planted. Grouped with hemlocks and firs, its light

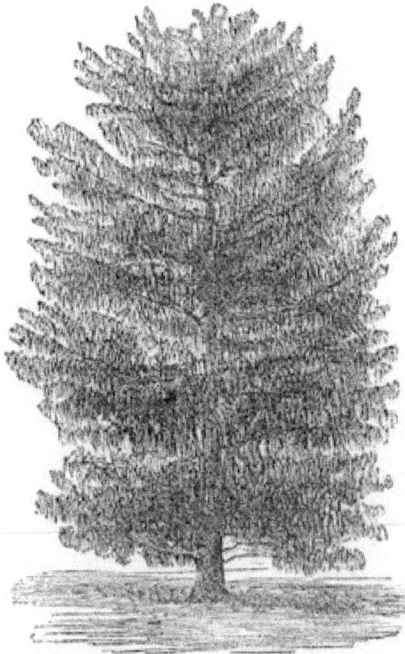

FIG. 4.—DECIDUOUS CYPRESS.

green foliage and airiness contrast beautifully with the more
somber shades of the evergreens.

DOGWOOD—*Cornus.*—The COMMON DOGWOOD (*cornus florida*)
abounds in almost all sections of the Middle States. Without
pretending rank as a tree, for it does not often grow above

twenty feet high, its profusion of pure white flowers in early spring have drawn attention of ornamental planters to it, until it is now sought for and planted by every landscapist of any taste. As a small tree to skirt the boundaries of evergreen groups, peeping out from among them with its snowy flowers in spring, and its brilliant red berries and dark red foliage in autumn, we have few equal to it.

There is a variegated-leaved variety also, with its leaves blotched with white, that when the plant is to stand with other deciduous trees is better because of the greater attraction created by its foliage; and there is also one, the *sanguinea*, with its young shoots of a bright scarlet color, that is extremely ornamental, whether planted by itself or against a relief of evergreens. The European dogwood (*mascula*) has small yellow flowers of no great beauty, but in the autumn its oval scarlet berries are very ornamental, and hang a long time on the tree.

ELM—*Ulmus.*—From the abundance of elms, everywhere native, over our country, and the almost perfect certainty of their living and growing freely when transplanted with ordinary care, it has become one of our most popular street and park trees. Gracefully elegant by reason of its long sweeping branches, and its loose pendant yet tufted masses of foliage, vigorous and almost lofty in its growth, and adapting itself as it were to all soils, wet or dry, clay or sand, the American white elm has no superior as a street or park tree, where it can be planted so as to give it room for development; but when planted, as it too often is, in small grounds, or on the sides of narrow streets or avenues where its limbs have to be lopped off or trimmed up, it is unsuited, because in so doing its beauty is destroyed, and the owner has only a long bare trunk where he might have had, with some other variety, a mass of foliage and beauty.

The red elm (*fulva*) is more upright in its growth than the

white, and does not attain as great size, but it is not as desirable
for planting in positions too confined for the white as the
European (*campestris*) or Scotch (*montana*) elms.

The European or English elm forms a lofty tree of less spreading habit than our white elm, and in retaining its foliage later,
extends apparently our season of summer.

As a shade tree it is more compact and dense in its foliage,
and therefore more suitable in the formation of masses or groups.

FIG. 5.—ENGLISH ELM.

A great number of varieties of this species occur among the
trees sold, because all are grown from seed, and the planter can
frequently select trees of a dozen different habits among those
offered by the dealer.

The Scotch or Wych elm is a variety nearer to our white elm
in its habits, but of less size and with a coarser foliage. It
appears to be suited with poor soils, where our white elm does

not flourish finely, and for use in planting on a rocky point or hill in connection with the birch it is the best.

For single trees on lawns of small extent, the cork-barked elm (*suberosa*) has claims that commend it to every planter. It is vigorous and hardy, foliage rich and dark, hanging late in autumn, and its branches and twigs covered with a fungous

FIG. 6.—JAPAN GINKO.

growth of a cork-like substance, so singular and curious as to attract attention and admiration. The foliage of all the elms in autumn is of a yellow tint.

GINKO—*Salisburia.*—The ginko is a tree of great botanical

curiosity because of its peculiar foliage, unlike that of any other tree or shrub, but nearest resembling the maiden-hair fern. In form it has generally a neat, regular, open, conical head, with its foliage on long petioles, giving it an airy and unique appearance that harmonizes well with buildings, but does not so well with masses or groups of other trees. It is perfectly hardy, and should be planted in every ground where a place

FIG. 7.—HORSE CHESTNUT.

can be arranged for it near to view, so that its character can be readily seen.

HORSE CHESTNUT—*Æsculus.*—For bordering the lines of straight avenues, and for public squares or town plots, where regularity and symmetry are desired rather than grandeur; for single lawn trees, and for limited use in grouping with the Scotch and Austrian pines, the horse chestnut is one of our best and most ornamental trees. While young it is a slow

grower, but when the trees get a height of eight or ten feet,
and are planted in a rich, deep, loamy soil which is best suited
to them, they grow rapidly, and soon form large, regular, round
symmetrical heads, clothed with a broad, clean foliage, and
decorated in spring with masses and clusters of white or red
blossoms according to the variety. By grafting the red-
blossoming variety (*rubicunda*) and the yellow (*glabra*) into
the principal portions of the top and center limbs of the
white (*hippocastanum*), a very beautiful and novel effect is produced, that when the tree stands alone on the lawn adds much
to its beauty.

There is now grown a variety of the *hippocastanum* with
double flowers that are very beautiful, like little roses. When
in full foliage and bloom the horse chestnut is one of the most
beautiful among ornamental trees; but it has one habit, that of
casting its foliage early in the fall, which we consider very
objectionable to its use near the house, as our summer season is
lessened in appearance nearly or quite a month thereby.

HICKORY—*Carya.*—The difficulty of transplanting the hickory
or white walnut tree has kept it from use in ornamental planting.
The trees are lofty and elegant when grown singly, and there
is a lively tint or character in their foliage which renders them
very pleasingly effective when found in groups or masses. They
are readily grown from the nut, and he who is just commencing
the planting of a new place should in this way introduce them
into his grounds.

LINDEN—*Tilia.*—Under the name of basswood our American
linden or lime tree is well known. Some years since that as
well as the European variety were so much preyed upon by
insects that their use in planting was almost abandoned. Of
late years, however, there is less injury from insects, and the
planting of lindens has again come into practice.

Of rapid growth, easily transplanted, full and flowing in its outline or form, its foliage broad and of a rich green, few of our native or exotic trees have more to recommend them than the linden. It prefers, and grows more vigorously in, a light and rich deep soil, but also grows well in even a poor sand or on a

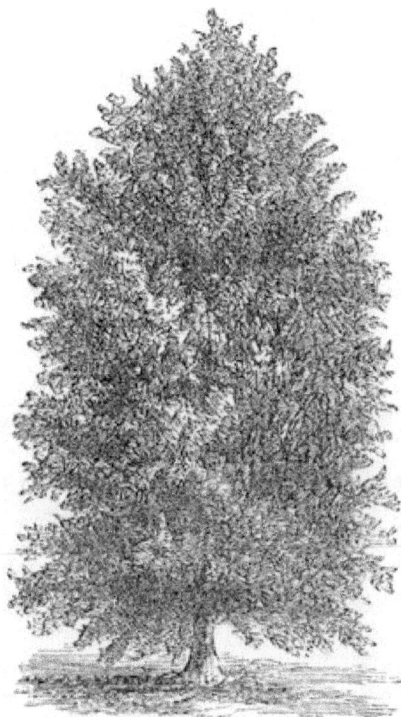

Fig. 8.—Linden.

clay, provided it is not wet. Its regular, uniform, but flowing form adapts it well to planting in grounds of the graceful school in composition, and also to avenues, streets, and public parks. In spring, its pale yellow clusters of flowers are quite ornamental;

and in autumn, its yellowish or yellowish brown foliage contrasts finely with many of the maples.

There are a number of varieties, the best of which we think is *alba* or the white-leaved linden, which has very broad foliage, deep green on the upper side and nearly white underneath, so that every breeze that rustles among it gives to it an airy and beautiful appearance. The European linden has smaller leaves than our American, and is perhaps more regular in its form; and there are also varieties of it, one with the young shoots quite red and one with them yellow, that are extremely ornamental in winter—the red especially—when grouped with evergreens, forming conspicuous lines. There are also fancy varieties, such as the fern-leaved, grape-leaved, etc., that are curious and pretty, and desirable for those who have plenty of room to display them.

Locust—*Robinia.*—We do not regard the locust as of much value for planting on roadsides, in parks, or private grounds. Its advocates have urged its rapid growth, but we have now so many trees of equally rapid growth, and so much better as a whole in themselves, that such recommendation can not avail. There are, however, positions in picturesque grouping where the locust with its long clusters of blossoms and airy lightness of foliage comes in admirably. For grounds of large extent, where variety as well as beauty serves to make up the scene, there are a number, such as the spreading (*horizontalis*), the crisp-leaved (*crispa*), the rose-flowered (*viscosa*), etc., that are interesting and deserving of room and care.

Under the common name of locust or honey locust is another, the THREE-THORNED ACACIA (*gleditschia triacanthos*), which should not be so lightly passed over. This is a tree that does not sucker; its branches are strong, rarely if ever breaking under the strongest gales of wind; assumes to itself the privilege of growing in many shapes, from that of a tall, branching, and lofty character, to one of almost horizontal form. In foliage it is light and open, feathery, and together with its wood studded with long pointed thorns, and seed pods of five or six inches in length, which hang on all winter, create for it a tree very desirable in the composition of groups, and also for roadsides or streets where only a partial, not deep, shade is desirable.

FIG. 9.—LARCH.

LARCH—*Larix.*—The European larch (*larix Europea*) is a tree almost indispensable in ornamental planting of grounds. Seemingly indifferent as to the nature of the soil, it grows with surprising rapidity in thin, poor, light sands, in wet, boggy loams, high rocky knolls, or in rich garden loam. Downing says, "It

2

can never be called a beautiful tree, so far as beauty consists in
smooth outlines ;" but in so saying we think he was in error, for
some of the most perfect outlines we ever saw in tree, regular
symmetrical cones from the ground upward, are to be found in
trees of the European larch where grown alone and in a light
dry soil. With Downing, however, we agree that it should be
sparingly planted in grounds where the graceful rather than the
picturesque style is designed to be created; but in the formation
of groups combined with the hemlock or the Norway spruce; in
planting a rocky knoll, or bordering some stream where its
drooping spray and swaying branches harmonize with the birch
or willow, and at the same time increase character and expression
by its spiry top, it is a tree of the highest value.

For street shades, or any position where its lower branches
have to be pruned away, it is entirely unsuited. Our American
larch, frequently called tamarack, is of slow growth when
planted in dry soil, as compared with the European, but in low,
wet situations it grows rapidly, and for picturesque effect is
even better, because of its more irregular habit.

The cones of the European variety are much larger than those
of the American, and when the tree is planted so that it can be
plainly seen, it is very beautiful, with its bright pink flowers
early in spring.

MAPLE—*Acer.*—All the maples are good as shade trees for
lawn or roadside, but among them the *rubrum*, red flowering, or
as generally termed scarlet maple, is most to be prized. Its red
flowers and leaves in early spring or beginning of summer; its
brilliant shades of red foliage in autumn, taken in connection with
its rapid growth and upright half spreading form, render it one
of the most ornamental of hardy trees. Although a native, and
abundant in many parts of our Northern and Middle States, one
or more trees of it should be found in all grounds of half an
acre or more in size. It may not be quite as rapid in growth as

the silver-leaved (*dasycarpum*), but it is more upright, and its branches less liable to be broken by heavy winds, and therefore more valuable as a street or park tree. The silver-leaved is, however, a very valuable variety, and where partially sheltered, or where it can have an opportunity to develop itself, it is one of the most graceful as well as lofty of the species. As the trees

Fig. 10.—Scarlet Maple.

are all grown from seeds, there is great variety of habit among them, some having almost as much of a drooping habit as the willow, others of a spreading open habit, similar to the American white elm. For light sandy soils the silver-leaved is perhaps the best, as even old trees growing in such soils seem to retain the vigor of youth, while the sugar maple, Norway, and some others make little progress after a few years, except in deep and strong soils.

The sugar maple (*saccharinum*) makes one of the most compact and regular of round-headed trees, forming a dense shade very agreeable to recline under in a hot summer's day. It is, however, a slow grower compared with the scarlet or silver-leaved, and should be planted only in rich, deep, and well-drained soils.

The moosewood or striped-barked maple is a small-growing variety, extremely pretty from its stripes of white and black upon the young green wood. It is adapted to the outside of groups, or to positions where a tree of only medium size is desired.

The large-leaved maple (*macrophyllum*) is as yet scarce, although introduced many years. It is of rapid growth, of a spreading, upright habit, and of great beauty from its immense size of foliage.

As a street shade, or for public parks, and especially as a tree to plant near the house where shade combined with stateliness and character are desired, the sycamore maple (*pseudo platanus*) has claims worthy of special notice. It is rapid in growth, with foliage broad and of a rich green, intermediate in appearance between the buttonwood or sycamore and the sugar maple. In autumn, when dying off, it becomes a rich golden yellow.

The Norway maple (*platanoides*) is another variety desirable. More upright, not as spreading as *pseudo platanus*, but with large, broad leaves, not of as rapid growth, nor forming so large a tree.

The variety commonly known as English maple (*campestris*) is of slow growth, forming a very stocky round-headed tree fifteen to twenty feet high, admirably suited for planting on some little rounded knoll or as the center of a group of low-growing shrubs.

There are also numerous fancy varieties, such as the tricolor, variegated-leaved, purple-leaved, cut-leaved, etc., etc., all of which are curious, and desirable in grounds of large extent; but in places where a limited number only can have place, the purple-leaved is the one particularly desirable. Its leaves are purplish underneath and pale green above when fully expanded; and at midsummer and thereafter until the fall of the leaf, every breeze that ruffles and disturbs them produces a singular and pleasing effect in contrast with the foliage of other varieties.

The ash-leaved maple or box elder (*negundo fraxinifolium*) is a very rapid-growing variety, of great beauty from its peculiar formed leaves and its pale green smooth young wood. It makes a large tree when grown in a deep, rich, moist soil; but in a light sandy loam or good garden soil, it forms a tree of medium size, that from its color of young wood in winter is exceedingly attractive and pleasing. It groups admirably with pines.

As a family, the maples have in themselves perhaps more of the elements for ornamental uses than any other; for when planted singly they are nearly all beautiful, some of them particularly so; and such is their diversity of foliage in spring and autumn, that a group of maples alone combines some of the most pleasing contrasts obtained in landscape adornment.

MAGNOLIA.—To this family, many varieties of which are the pride of our Southern States, too little attention is given by the majority of tree planters; whether it is that good plants are difficult to be obtained, or whether it is because the trees are rather sensitive and unwilling to be carelessly and negligently handled when transplanting, we find few planters make room for them on their lists or in their grounds; but how any landscapist can form an extensive group of evergreens and deciduous trees without using magnolias, is beyond our comprehension. In our experience, we have found no difficulty when transplanting, provided we kept the roots from cold drying winds or clear

burning suns; exposure to either of which, by reason of their
soft, spongy texture, is injurious, and often destructive of life.
Of the varieties all are beautiful, but some are not perfectly
hardy when grown in our Northern States. A sandy loamy soil
suits them best; but if it is strictly dry, the trees of some varieties,
as *macrophylla*, etc., are liable to die out in from five to ten
years. We prefer to make our soil, when not naturally suited,
by digging a place three to four feet deep and eight to ten feet

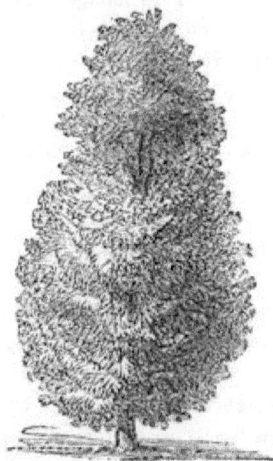

Fig. 11.—Magnolia Acuminata.

diameter, and fill it with light, rich, fresh top soil drawn from
the woods.

The magnolia *acuminata*, or cucumber-tree as it is frequently
called, is very upright and regular, almost cone-like in its form,
and for backgrounds or the center of groups one of the most
desirable of all deciduous trees. It is also one of the very best
trees for parks or public grounds, as it is almost if not entirely
free from insects, and grows very rapidly while young. For

street trees, where there is liability of injury to its bark or body, we do not advise it.

The *macrophylla* or large-leaved magnolia grows so rapidly while young, that in our Northern States it is comparatively tender, and requires to be protected for eight or ten years, or until it seems to have arrived at comparative maturity, after which we have found it perfectly hardy. In our Southern States, or all south of Washington, it is one of the most beautiful of the many beautiful trees of that semi-tropical region.

The magnolia *cordata* is another Southern variety, but per-

Fig. 12.—MAGNOLIA GLAUCA.

fectly hardy in most sections of the Northern States. It makes a tree of medium size, and is not desirable except for large grounds or collections. The *auriculata* is a variety very similar to the *acuminata* in general appearance, not quite as vigorous, and does not make as large a tree, and for parks or pleasure-grounds, where beauty, not a botanical specimen, is the point sought for, it is not equal in value to the *acuminata*.

The *glauca* or swamp magnolia is almost a sub-evergreen, often retaining its foliage until January, even in our Northern States.

Unless grafted or budded on the acuminata, it is only a dwarf, growing from six to twenty feet high—more like a bush than a tree. In moist, cool situations it often flowers all the season, June to September; but in open, exposed, sunny locations it flowers but once, in spring. The fragrance of its flowers, together with the rich, glossy, pale-green foliage and young shoots, form for it a shrub tree that were it to be now newly introduced, would cause an excitement rarely known in the arboricultural world. There are a number of sub-varieties, as

FIG. 13.—MAGNOLIA CONSPICUA.

longifolia, *Gordoniana*, *Thompsoniana*, etc., better, because larger in foliage, and perhaps a little stronger in growth; but their hardihood in all situations remains yet to be tested.

Magnolia *tripetela*, called the umbrella tree, when grown north of Philadelphia, seldom acquires much size; and although perfectly hardy where it has a season warm enough to ripen its wood, yet the main stem often dies when it has acquired a height of twelve to fifteen feet and a size of four to six inches diameter; the crown and root, however, do not die, but the root sends up several sprouts, making the plant rather a bush than a tree. Its flowers are very fragrant, and as a tree to group with mountain ash on the outskirts of pines, it is one of the most effective. Of the Chinese varieties, the magnolia *conspicua* and *soulangeana* are the most generally known; both are good; but if we were to select one, it would be the *soulangeana*, because it is a more rapid grower, and its flowers appear to escape injury from late spring frosts better than the *conspicua*. Both are perfectly hardy, form spreading, round-headed trees of middle size, and should always be placed where they will form the foreground of a group of evergreens, on account of their flowers being produced early in spring or before the growth of their leaves. There is a variety described as *Norbertiana*, with habit and growth of the conspicua, but having flowers of a dark purplish color and very fragrant. And another is described as *Lenne*, with flowers like the soulangeana, but of more than twice their size.

Magnolia *purpurea* and *gracilis* are both shrubs, and will be noticed in their place, we here remarking that their planting and arrangement as undergrowths or foregrounds to the conspicua and soulangeana are productive of a happy effect.

MULBERRY—*Morus.*—Although not a tree of the highest beauty, yet the native mulberry is not inelegant; and wherever it can be grown successfully, the great value of its fruit adds much to recommend its adoption in forming groups of deciduous trees, as it harmonizes well with the linden, catalpa, and some others of round heads and broad foliage. In some sections, however, of our Northern States, the trees are tender; and although not often killed entirely, they are frequently injured so much in the branches as to greatly impair their regularity and beauty. The variety now well known as "Downing's Everbearing," raised from seed some years ago by Charles Downing, Newburg, N. Y., is as hardy as any; and as its fruit is large and

2*

fine, with the addition of blossoming and ripening a long time in succession, it is the best to plant. A rich, deep, loamy, well-drained soil is best suited to the tree; and when possible, a position sheltered from severe winds as well as strong suns in winter, aids materially in its hardihood and productiveness. In our Northern States it can not be advised for street or park planting, but in the Southern and Middle States both the *morus* and *Broussonetia* are valuable trees for such uses.

FIG. 14.—MOUNTAIN ASH.

MOUNTAIN ASH — *Pyrus.* — Among professional as well as amateur planters, the European mountain ash is a deserved and general favorite. Its white flowers in the month of May, profusely spread out over its surface in thick, flat clusters, followed by bunches of round scarlet berries in autumn, and which if not destroyed or eaten by birds often hang on a great part of winter, make the tree highly ornamental when planted by itself, and still more so when it is the foreground of a cluster of spruces or pines. It does not grow of sufficient size for a street or park shade tree, but for small grounds and for narrow roads and paths in cemeteries it is admirably adapted. It may be, and usually is, grown with a single stem, with its branches thrown out at three or four feet from the ground; but on lawns or grass plots, and as connected with evergreens, it is much handsomer if permitted to throw out a number of stems directly from the crown, as represented in our engraving.

The American variety (*pyrus Americana*) does not make quite as large a tree as the European, but is more abundant in the numbers of its flowers and fruits; the latter, however, are not quite as brilliant in color.

The sorb or service tree (*pyrus sorbus*) and the white beam tree (*pyrus aria*) are two additional varieties of occasional use; the former because of the tree attaining a larger size, and therefore better suited to some positions, and also to the fact that its fruit, when frosted and in a state of partial decay, is by some regarded as pleasantly palatable.

The white beam grows very compact, and its leaves being deep green on the upper side and nearly white underneath, when ruffled by the wind present at times a pleasing contrast with the clear green of evergreens and other trees with which it may be grouped.

A variety of mountain ash (*quercifolia*) introduced within a few years past, with foliage resembling the oak, claims, however, a first place when only one tree is to be planted. Its growth is as rapid as any variety, form very regular and symmetrical, with foliage lobed like the oak, and bearing flowers and fruit quite as freely as any of the varieties.

There are also a number of other sorts, as the elder-leaved, pear-leaved, golden-striped, etc., that are each curious and beautiful in themselves, and especially valuable in all places of large extent.

The mountain ash will grow freely in any soil, but it will not bear much cutting away of limbs or branches.

OAK—*Quercus.*—The oak is the tree of song and tradition; the poet, painter, historiographer, and tourist all lend their aid to depict its beauty in association, in light and shade of landscape, together with its great value as a timber and food tree; and were we writing an essay upon the beauty of light and shade in scenery, stateliness and grandeur of tree, etc., it should receive from us unqualified praise. But as it is, we are only outlining brief descriptions of popular trees for planting on street sides, and in public and private parks of the United States, and the truth compels us to write, that however much grand old oaks may be admired, their use, for ornamenting lawns, or for producing cooling shades on roadsides or grandeur in parks, as yet has been very limited, and they can not claim to be classed as popular in comparison with the elm and maple.

The difficulty of transplanting the oak after it has acquired a suitable size for position on the roadside, etc., has undoubtedly prevented its adoption in many places where the taste of the planter would have otherwise chosen it; and this very difficulty has contributed to keep it out of most dealers' catalogues. Those who desire to plant it, we advise to select the early autumn, just as soon as the foliage is ripe, even before it falls, as the best time for its removal. It has deep and strong taproots, and they must, as far as possible, be obtained in its removal; and when transplanted, the ground should be at once thoroughly saturated with water.

With all its stateliness and grandeur; its boldness and freedom of outline; its great variety and irreverence to the rules of symmetry and regularity, making plantations of it when of age so expressive and commanding, we have an impression that for our American wants, our American people have appreciated it correctly, for with all its grandeur and beauty, many of the varieties have the habit of retaining their dead brown leaves, hanging in dirty masses all winter, marring rather than adorning the landscape.

Downing says of it, that "to arrive at its highest perfection, ample space on every side must be allowed," and where such position can be given it in public or private grounds, we should plant it; but in small suburban and village home grounds there are no such places, and their owners must be content with trees of a less historical or poetical interest.

Of the varieties most ornamental, we enumerate the rock chestnut oak—*Quercus prinus monticola;* chestnut white oak— *Q. prinus palustris;* yellow oak—*Q. prinus acuminata;* pin oak —*Q. palustris;* willow oak—*Q. phellos;* 'overcup white oak—*Q. macrocarpa;* scarlet oak—*Q. coccinea;* and English oak, *Q. robur.*

The live oak—*Q. virens* of the South—is beautiful, and there can be grown as a park tree; but it will not endure the climate of the Northern States. A very interesting and curious tree is the cork oak—*Q. suber.* Its branches are covered with a cork-like exerescence that gives to the tree a very unique and singular appearance.

Where the proprietor of a place has a desire for oaks, our advice is for him to prepare the ground in the several places where the trees are to stand, and then plant the acorns, staking around the same to prevent injury to the young plant. If the soil is made deep and rich, the plants will grow very rapidly, sometimes making four to five feet in a single season.

OSAGE ORANGE—*Maclura.*—The osage orange is generally grown for the purpose of forming hedges, but when grown singly it makes a tree of medium size, with a regular round head, covered with clean glossy foliage and rich golden fruit, in appearance resembling the orange of commerce.

It is admirably suited as a lawn tree for small plots, and for grouping with other round-headed deciduous trees of larger growth. In this latter position it should always be on the outside of the group. It grows very rapidly while young, but after attaining a height of fifteen to twenty feet its growth is more moderate. It is a tree well suited for planting on the narrow avenues of cemeteries, and for bold, rugged fronts of rocky banks; but is of too small size for roadsides or park avenues.

Upon lawns of large extent, an elegant monster shrub tree

FIG. 15.—OSAGE ORANGE.

can be created from the osage orange by annually heading it back near to the ground until it is induced to send up a dozen leading stems instead of one; these again, as they grow, want heading back more or less from year to year, until the plant becomes a gigantic bush rather than a tree.

The tree is easily and, generally, very successfully transplanted; and although it grows most vigorously in a deep, rich, light loam, yet it will grow freely in any soil not wet.

POPLAR—*Populus.*—Many of the poplars are valuable trees in

the decoration of scenery, but their use must be with moderation, because of a sameness and formality belonging to many of them that makes their too free use give a monotonous and

FIG. 16.—LOMBARDY POPLAR.

wearying character. They are all of very rapid growth, easily transplanted, and some of them form trees of immense size.

For the purpose of giving variety and spirit to grounds where the round-headed trees are most abundant, one or two Lombardy poplars—*populus dilatata*—may be introduced with great effect;

and again, two or three trees of it, planted directly in the rear
of the dwelling, furnish a relief and background, adding greatly
to the appearance as a picture. When distant views are desired,
permission to plant one or two Lombardy poplars at or near the
point will serve to attract the eye, and in themselves add an air
of animation to the scene. It should never be planted as a
foreground tree, or near water, or in low grounds; and as an
avenue tree, its stiff, regular form creates monotony that becomes
tiresome.

The balsam poplar—*balsamifera*—and the balm of Gilead
poplar—*candicans*—very much resemble each other in their rapid
growth and spreading habit; but their foliage is entirely distinct, the former having lanceolate oval leaves, while the latter
has very large, broad, heart-shaped foliage, and is much the
most desirable. Both are good for roadside trees or broad
avenues, and their use in filling up low grounds or bordering
streams of water is always satisfactory. As a background tree,
covering and shading barns or other farm-buildings, the balm
of Gilead is very effective.

The silver poplar—*abele*—is a tree remarkable for its silvery
white underside of foliage, that at every rustle of the wind
gives it, when seen from a distance, very much the appearance
of a tree covered with white blossoms.

It was once pretty generally planted in lawns and groups, but
the disposition which it has to sucker makes it extremely objectionable for such positions. As a tree to make conspicuous some
particular high point, or, where possible, to form the foreground
of a group of dark firs, it is very desirable, and always effective.
All the poplars bear the smoke and dust of cities with great
indifference; and where pavements will serve to keep down the
suckers, they are desirable, because of their extremely rapid
growth, exceeding perhaps that of any other tree.

PEPPERIDGE—*Nyssa.*—The sour gum or pepperidge tree is

generally, when wild, found growing in moist or wet land, but it will thrive in any good deep soil. The tree has no particular claims to beauty in its habit of growth, but from its dark green glossy foliage in summer, and the brilliant fiery tinge which it takes on when ripening its leaves, it is extremely valuable for forming groups in the picturesque style. A single tree of it even, standing at some distance from the house, and where its brilliant autumn tints can be readily seen, often forms for

FIG. 17.—PERSIMMON.

weeks a feature of beauty surpassing that of any other on the place.

PERSIMMON—*Diospyros.*—The persimmon or Virginia date plum makes an open, irregular, half round-headed, rather erect tree of pleasing character and of a medium size, that fits it well for grounds of limited extent. It groups well with the English elm, the bird cherry, and others; and when the value of its fruit is regarded, deserves a place in almost all grounds. In the southern sections of Illinois, Missouri, etc., there are varieties of it that ripen their fruits long before frost; but the wild trees of its northern limits generally produce a very austere fruit, quite uneatable until after mellowed by frost.

It is a good tree for planting in cemeteries, and for rocky positions where a light, airy character is desired to be retained. Any good soil will answer for it, although it grows most vigorously in rich, deep, rather moist loams.

PAULOWNIA—*Paulownia.*—There are few localities in the Northern States where the paulownia can command much attention, for while the tree may remain uninjured, the flower-buds are almost invariably destroyed by the cold. Southward, where the catalpa flourishes, the paulownia is a desirable acquisition. In growth and habit it much resembles the catalpa, but its flowers are of a purple or bluish lilac color. For situations and climates suited to the catalpa, the paulownia will be found alike adapted.

SASSAFRAS—*Laurus.*—As an open foreground tree for groups, the glossy deep green foliage of the sassafras, and its irregular swaying branches, make it especially desirable. Even while young, the peculiar cracked and gray of its bark give an appearance of age, to some extent adding antiquity of character to a new place.

TULIP TREE—*Liriodendron.*—The tulip or whitewood is one of the most beautiful and stately of our native trees. It is a rapid grower, erect, yet partially spreading, forming a regular, even, conically rounded head, with a large, broad, rich, glossy leaf, and smooth, clean bark. Like the magnolias, its roots are soft, and do not bear exposure to dry winds or sun when transplanting, and the planter must use care and attention in their removal. For avenues for public or private parks, for single trees upon lawns, and especially for shade near the house, there is no tree its superior. In the month of June its profusion of large tulip-like yellow flowers give it a richness and beauty all unlike that of any other tree, and to our view only equaled by some of the magnolias. It requires a dry and deep rich soil, in order to develop its greatest beauty; but it will thrive in any good loam where there is a perfect drainage.

WALNUT—*Juglans.*—Under the name of walnut we have the European walnut, and the black walnut of our native forests.

The European walnut, perhaps most commonly known as Madeira nut, although largely planted in France and Germany for its fruit, has not received much attention in this country. In our Northern States it is not quite hardy. As an ornamental tree, in a climate suited to it, it makes a pleasing variety because of the contrast in its foliage with that of most other trees; but as it casts its foliage early in the season, it can not be commended for planting except in grounds of large extent and variety.

The black walnut—*juglans nigra*—makes a very rapid growth, and becomes a very large and spreading tree. For broad streets in the country, or for massing in grounds of great extent, it is desirable; but when there is only a limited space of say an acre or two to be planted, or a narrow avenue, it should not be used. As a single tree, where it can have space, the light and shade created by its foliage, and its sweeping, bold ramifications of outline, give to it an expression of beauty; but it must have room.

WILLOW—*Salix.*—There is a large genus of willows, all of narrow leaves and slender branches or spray. Few of them, however, are calculated for general introduction for ornamental planting. The weeping varieties will be found treated of under their appropriate head. Of the others, the golden—*salix vitellina*, with its bright yellow bark, is a tree. deserving of adoption wherever it can be grouped with the birch, wild cherry, or trees of a like character. It should be used, however, very sparingly, one or two being sufficient for grounds of even large extent. Occasionally a position is found where a single tree becomes very beautiful, from its rich shade of spray in winter, and its

peculiar green foliage in summer.   In ordinary grounds it forms
only a tree of moderate size; but in rich strong soils, and near
water, it makes a large spreading tree.   It is not at all suited
for planting in parks or for bordering avenues or streets, but
may be sometimes introduced in cemeteries, and especially
because that it will bear to have its roots and branches cut back
to any extent almost without appearing to affect its health or
vigor.

The white willow—*salix alba*—has of late years been frequently
used in some portions of the Western States for forming hedges
and screens.   It is of rapid growth, and when permitted to grow
by itself, forms quite a large tree.   It also may be sparsely introduced where light and airy groups are desired.

CHAPTER III.

WEEPING DECIDUOUS TREES.

WITHIN a few years the popular taste has been largely turned to the introduction of drooping trees as objects of graceful beauty, harmonizing with the smoothness and verdure of a lawn, or the high keeping and neatness of a pleasure-garden. Indeed, to such an extent has this taste prevailed, that the very object aimed at in their introduction has been often defeated by a too free use of them, as well as by their arrangement in masses, when their side branches—which are their peculiar beauty—are intermingled or hidden entirely, and by their too heedless distribution on all sides.

Drooping trees, like water fountains, are dangerous in the hands of those who attempt their use in the decoration of grounds without possessing a considerable knowledge and good taste in the composition of a landscape. Gracefulness and elegance being the prominent characteristics of drooping trees, they are shown to best advantage either singly or in wide yet tasteful groups, on lawns or borders, where symmetrical art, rather than the natural picturesque, is sought to be embodied as the leading feature. Where bold expression is desired, they are entirely unfitted; and when planted mixed indiscriminately with those of upright, round-headed forms, their individual character is lost. Placed on the borders of groups, at sufficient distance to enable them to exhibit their peculiar habits and develop freely their forms, many of the drooping trees may be used effectively, provided the group of which they form a part is composed of trees with similar pensile, although not so distinct, habits of foliage or spray, as exhibited in the American elm, black birch, or wild cherry.

For planting on the borders of ponds, or streams of running water, or as symbols of sympathy between the living and the dead in cemeteries, they are all valuable; and with judicious knowledge of their expansion in growth, to arrange them on lots or in positions suitable to their future lives, they can not be too much used.

FIG. 18.—EUROPEAN WEEPING ASH.

The EUROPEAN WEEPING ASH—*Fraxinus excelsior pendula.*— This is one of the oldest varieties of weeping trees known, and more extensively planted than any. It was discovered about the middle of the last century, growing in a field in England. The branches are stiff, and can not be called graceful in their downward curves; but its clean, glossy foliage and its very rapid growth render it one of the most valuable, especially for forming arbors.

The GOLD-BARKED WEEPING ASH—*Aurea pendula*.—This is a singular variety, because of its bright, golden-yellow bark, which gives it a striking appearance when devoid of foliage. In growth and habit it is similar to the last-named.

The LENTISCUS-LEAVED WEEPING ASH—*Lentiscifolia pendula*. —A tree of later introduction than the two preceding. Equally rapid in its growth, but with branches more slender and graceful. It is much the most beautiful in appearance, but in some

FIG. 19.—WEEPING BEECH.

locations is not perfectly hardy, losing occasional branches, which destroy its symmetry. There are two other varieties of weeping ash, viz., the gold-striped bark weeping, with variegated foliage, and the weeping black, with very dark-green foliage. We have never seen either of them of any size, and therefore can not speak of their values.

The WEEPING BEECH—*Fagus pendula*.—This we consider the king of all the drooping trees. It is perfectly hardy, grows freely and rapidly in almost any soil, and forms one of the most graceful and picturesque yet unique trees. Its branches are thrown out irregularly, while its spray is long, descending

almost perpendicularly downward. For creating a distinct,
strongly-marked, and attractive feature for universal admiration
on the skirts of a lawn, it has no superior.

The EUROPEAN WEEPING BIRCH—*Betula pendula.*—A tree of
rapid, upright, spreading growth, that while young exhibits
very little of a drooping habit, and even when old is not marked

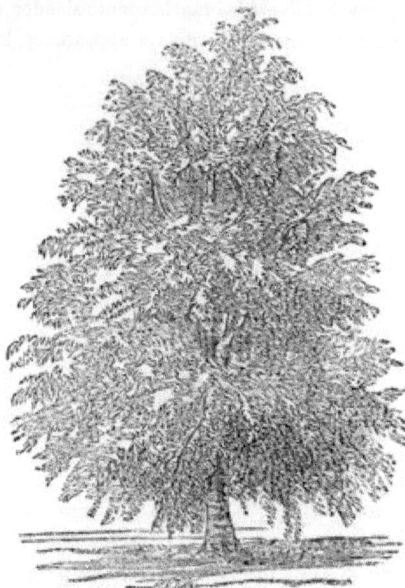

FIG. 20.—CUT-LEAVED WEEPING BIRCH.

as a weeper, like many others. It is, however, very graceful,
and as it increases in years presents more and more of the pensile
features that, combined with its delicate foliage, make it a
charming tree for grouping with others of a like slender spray
and airy foliage.

The CUT-LEAVED WEEPING BIRCH—*Betula lasciniata pendula.*
—An elegant, erect tree, similar to the preceding, but with

more slender drooping branches, and with delicately cut leaves, that attract and please every observer.

The EVER-FLOWERING WEEPING CHERRY—*Cerasus semper florens.*—This is of comparatively recent introduction, and forms a charming tree of a decided drooping habit, and producing a succession of flowers and fruit all the season.

The DWARF WEEPING CHERRY—*Cerasus pumila.*—For small grounds, points on the outskirts of a group, or other positions where a limited space only can be allowed, this is one of the prettiest of weepers. Its branches are slender and decidedly

FIG. 21.—DWARF WEEPING CHERRY.

drooping, growing freely, and forming a charmingly graceful little round head.

The SCOTCH WEEPING ELM—*Ulmus montana pendula.*—The habit of this variety of weeping elm is very irregular, sometimes spreading its branches fan-like, at others drooping them almost perpendicularly downward. It is a tree of rapid growth, with an abundance of coarse, heavy, dark foliage, that is suitable for positions where it can have abundance of room, and where it will be viewed at some little distance. This is the variety generally found in the nurseries; but there are two varieties of more recent introduction, which we consider superior in growth, as they certainly are in symmetry of form.

3

One of these, the SCAMPSTON, droops its branches very distinctly and regularly, giving the tree a symmetrical form, almost as regular as if it had been trained, trimmed, and tied from time to time by the hands of a skillful gardener. The other variety is called the CAMPERDOWN, and differs from the Scampston in its branches, having a less tendency to regular drooping, and its foliage not being quite as abundant.

There are also two varieties, called the rough-leaved weeping and the Hertfordshire weeping, that are not counted as desirable

FIG. 22.—SCAMPSTON WEEPING ELM.

as those previously named. There is also one called the small-leaved weeping, which is said to be very pretty and distinct.

The WHITE-LEAVED WEEPING LINDEN—*Tilia alba pendula*.—Although a tree of slender drooping shoots, it is not a weeper after the style of the weeping willow; but, like the birch, as it increases in years, it exhibits a drooping habit, that combined with the silvery character given to its foliage when stirred by the breeze, by their white under-surface, makes it one of the most attractive and graceful of lawn trees. It is of rapid growth, and deserves to be planted in every place of any extent.

The WEEPING MOUNTAIN ASH—*Pyrus aucuparia pendula.*— This is a rapid growing, beautiful variety of the mountain ash. Its long, pendulous branches, with their white flowers in spring, and red berries thereafter, make it very beautiful and attractive. Those who . plant it should, however, remember that it is extremely liable to be attacked by the borer, and unless closely

FIG. 23.—WHITE-LEAVED WEEPING LINDEN.

watched, the tree will be found destroyed ere the owner is aware.

The WEEPING POPLAR—*Populus tremula pendula.*—One of the most rapid growing of all the weepers, and while young, its decidedly pendulous branches, neat and pretty foliage, make it especially desirable. As it increases in years, however, it puts on more of an erect habit, until at times its upper limbs present very small indications of a weeping habit. For large grounds, or groups of weepers, or as a tree to plant a little back from the margin of lakes or large ponds, it is desirable; but for small grounds, or for cemetery lots, where we have of late occasionally seen it planted, it will not prove as satisfactory and pleasing as many others.

The WEEPING SOPHORA—*Sophora Japonica pendula.*—The smooth, dark-green, and very pendulous branches, together with its pinnate leaves, give to this tree a very elegant appearance. It is a rapid grower, but does not form a very large or spreading head, and is therefore an admirable tree for grounds or positions

FIG. 24.—WEEPING MOUNTAIN ASH.

of limited extent. Although we occasionally find trees of it that have stood the winters of years perfectly in our Northern States, yet it is unfortunately a little liable to be injured by extremes of temperature, and probably from this cause has not been as extensively planted as its beauty would seem to merit. Where it can be grown perfectly free from winter's injury, it may be counted as one of a choice collection.

The WEEPING WILLOW—*Salix Babylonica.*—Our old, common, and well-known weeping willow, like too many other trees that

are familiar to all, is neglected, yet it deserves the attention of
every planter of weeping trees. It may be that because we have
so often watched the willow droop and dip its branches in the
water of some stream or lake, seeming as it were to sympathize
with and kiss the sparkling drops that it disturbed as the gentle
winds swayed its tresses of light and elegant foliage, we have
come to love it, and regard no water landscape as complete
without the graceful flowing lines of the old Babylonian willow.
From long usage it has come to be associated with either water
or the sadness of life—in the one case indicative of a marshy
region or stream of water, in the other of the last resting-place

FIG. 25.—AMERICAN, OR FOUNTAIN WILLOW.

of friends once on earth. Beautiful as it is in itself, however,
these very associations preclude its introduction into almost any
suburban or even extended country place. By the side of a
spring at the foot of a hill, or bordering a stream where crossed
by a bridge, or in large grounds, shading almost entirely from
view the under-gardener's house, are some of the places where its
position produces a satisfactory effect; but if planted near where
art and architecture have combined to give a tone of grandeur
and magnificence, its form of outline and waving spray seem
rather to weaken than add to the appearance of cultivation and
refinement

The AMERICAN, OR FOUNTAIN WILLOW — *Salix Americana pendula.* — A variety with very slender, graceful branches, which droop perpendicularly, like so many cords, that, taken with its light and comparatively sparse foliage, form for it one of the most airy and pleasing weepers in the whole list. It is admirably adapted for planting upon small lots in cemeteries.

The KILMARNOCK WILLOW — *Salix caprea pendula.* — We know of no one weeping tree that in the same length of

FIG. 26. — KILMARNOCK WILLOW.

time has become so universally known and so extensively planted. Its foliage, large, glossy, and abundant, its pendulous, close, and regular habit, with its brown-colored branches, that are almost hidden within its foliage, render it one of the most distinctive as well as graceful trees that have been for many years added to our collections. It is perfectly hardy, and almost unlike anything else, seems to adapt itself to almost any position, whether as a point tree to define a road, a specimen of beauty and attraction on a small lawn or garden plot, or as an outline to some more aspiring tree of a similar drooping caste.

The WEEPING ACACIA—*Robinia tortuosa pendula.*—This is a variety of the locust, with long, drooping, irregular branches, too large in size to form with the light open leaf, which it has, a tree of much beauty. It is singular, and in some rocky positions is well suited; but it has not sufficient beauty for planting, as we have often seen done, near where it has to be passed in daily walking to and from the house.

The WEEPING LARCH—*Larix pendula.*—We have seen people go into almost ecstasies over this peculiar weeper; but to our taste, its graceful drooping spray is destroyed by its grotesque irregular habit, sometimes branching off at one point eight or ten feet almost horizontally, destroying all symmetry, which is a part of grace. For creating a picturesque effect upon a rocky side-hill, or near a water-course or pond springing out from a bold bank, its introduction would be desirable; but for placing upon a smooth, well-kept lawn where all is symmetrically beautiful, its use creates a contrast too great for harmony.

The WEEPING THORN.—There are several varieties of weeping thorns—*crætegus*—all of them pretty, and well suited for planting on small lawns or in cemeteries. The *pyracantha folia pendula* and *rosea pendula* are, perhaps, two of the best. They are improved by clipping, and when in flower are peculiarly interesting and beautiful. Their stems should be carefully watched, as, otherwise, an insect is liable to bore into and destroy them.

CHAPTER IV.

DECIDUOUS TREES WITH COLORED OR VARIEGATED FOLIAGE.

THE use of trees with variegated foliage is becoming popular. Their introduction into groups may occasionally be admissible, but as a rule they should be planted only where they can stand alone and develop themselves fully.

In writing of trees in previous pages, we have occasionally named one or more varieties, but for the more ready use of the reader will here recapitulate somewhat of what we have written, and add thereto remarks upon other sorts. Of those having purple or purplish-colored foliage, the beech, elm, and maple all are desirable and very beautiful for single lawn trees, where they can have room to develop themselves fully in growth, and where they can be viewed at some little distance.

The purple-leaved filbert and barberry are shrubs, conspicuous for planting where trees can not have room, and where variety and peculiarity of foliage will assist in making up the beauty of the grounds.

The spotted or variegated-leaved trees are more admissible in groups; and when their growth is free and healthy, serve to add variety with beauty; but, as we have before said, it is better 'to plant them singly and as features of special attraction.

For this purpose the golden-leaved beech, variegated-leaved cherry, variegated-leaved horse-chestnut, silver striped-leaved maple, and variegated-leaved plum are among the best.

CHAPTER V.

EVERGREEN TREES.

THE use of evergreens is becoming yearly more and more appreciated, both as effective in ornamental planting and as an item of practical economy in the matter of hedges and screens for protection of half hardy plants, orchards, or buildings from cold and harsh winds and storms.

In ornamental planting, their use is often very imperfectly understood, and many places are rendered gloomy and dark from their too free use in the foreground, or immediately about the house. There is a great deal of beauty in evergreens, but as a class for effective scenery creative of varied beauty, they have not the qualities that are embraced in the changing character from month to month of deciduous trees. For perfect scenery, however, covering the entire year, it would be impossible to dispense with evergreens. If used judiciously in arrangement, sparingly in the foreground, and using those of the lightest and most vivid shades of green in foliage, grouping them at the same time with mountain ash, euonymus or strawberry tree, etc., with their red clusters of fruit in winter, and massing the back-ground with varieties of dark foliage, great effect may be produced, and a pleasant life-like character given to grounds that otherwise in the winter season would be barren and dreary.

Some few years since, many regarded the transplanting of evergreens as one of the difficult items in arboriculture, requiring the skill and experience of a practical gardener. It was also counted unsafe to move them except at particular seasons

3*

of the year, or with balls of earth attached, and a few planters yet hold to these early views; but those of more practice find that it is no more difficult to transplant an evergreen when taken from the nursery than to perform the same operation with any deciduous tree.   It is true there are exceptions among evergreens, some proving more difficult than others, but the instances or kinds are not more numerous than with deciduous trees.

In transplanting, it is only requisite to remember that the tree has its leaves on, and that there is consequently a constant demand upon the roots for evaporation, and therefore it will not do to permit them to get dry. With small-sized trees, a root nearly corresponding with the top is generally procured when the trees have been rightly grown in the nursery, and cutting in the top is unnecessary; but in the case of removal of trees six feet or more in height, unless extraordinary care is taken, a great reduction of root is the result, and then it is advisable always to shorten in the length of the branches corresponding with the apparent loss of roots the tree has sustained.

A very great variety of evergreens have been introduced during the past fifteen or twenty years, but of them few have proved of a hardihood or beauty to command notice as trees for popular use; and as in these pages we write for the general public rather than for a few amateurs, we shall only describe such as may be safely depended upon in all locations.

THE WHITE PINE.   *Pinus strobus.*—The White or Weymouth Pine is common in various parts of the Union, and deserving of a first place in every collection. It is of rapid growth, beautiful in every stage, from a small plant of one foot high to that of a stately tree towering one hundred or more feet in the air, and swaying its horizontal tiers of branches and tufts of airy light-green foliage to the breeze. When grown in strong soil it acquires a thick, compact form; but in soils of a gravelly or sandy nature, somewhat dry and poor, its shoots and trunk harmonize in their length and openness to the airy light cast of its foliage, and it there becomes one of the most beautiful of evergreens in its graceful tapering form and easy broken outline. For grouping with the larch, birch, etc., it is one of the most appropriate among evergreens; and for planting in close

FIG. 27.—THE WHITE PINE.

proximity to buildings, or points toward which it desired to direct attention, it is particularly well suited. As a hedge or screen plant it bears the shears well, and forms a wall second only to the hemlock or Norway spruce.

THE BHOTAN PINE. *Pinus excelsa.*—This variety resembles
the white pine, except that its foliage is longer and its branches
somewhat pendulous, but in our Northern States it can not be
regarded as perfectly hardy. In the southern Middle States it is
one of the finest among evergreens, and should be freely planted.

FIG. 28.—BHOTAN PINE.

THE YELLOW PINE. *Pinus mitis.*—This is a very handsome
variety when well grown, but while young its growth is quite
slow, and on that account it is rarely grown or planted. Its
foliage is a dark rich green, long and flexible.

THE AUSTRIAN PINE. *Pinus Austriaca.*—The Austrian Pine
in rich deep soils forms one of the most dense trees of the whole
pine family. It is of rapid growth, with rich deep blue-green
foliage, that for backgrounds or masses is admirably suited.

As a single tree, also, upon a lawn, it is always beautiful; and, when the scenery will admit, groups of this pine with the tulip tree, mountain ash, dogwood, etc., are exceedingly effective.

There is a Southern Pine—*Pinus Australis*—native of our

FIG. 29.—THE AUSTRIAN PINE.

Southern States, that has leaves much longer than the Austriaca, and of a lighter more yellow green. It, however, is not hardy in the middle Northern States unless shielded, or surrounded, in fact, with other evergreens. South, where it is hardy, few varieties surpass it in beauty.

THE RUSSIAN PINE. *Pinus rigensis.*—This is a variety claimed by some writers to be so like unto the Scotch Pine—*P. sylvestris* —as not to be worthy of rank as a species. Trees, however, that we have imported and grown are so entirely different from that variety, that we must claim it deserving a special rank. The tree is of about as rapid growth as the Austrian, with its

FIG. 30.—THE RUSSIAN PINE.

limbs and branches more loose and open or longer spaced, while its foliage is more in tufts, much longer than the Austrian, and of a lighter more yellowish green, very bright and clear. It is nearer to Benthamiana than any other variety with which we have had opportunity to compare it. In groups or masses with the Scotch, Corsican, and Austrian, it forms yet another shade.

and we have found its use a valuable addition in producing effect.

THE BANKSIAN PINE.   *Pinus Banksiana.*—This variety is classed as a scrub pine of low slow growth and little value, and so we regarded it twenty-five years ago, when we procured

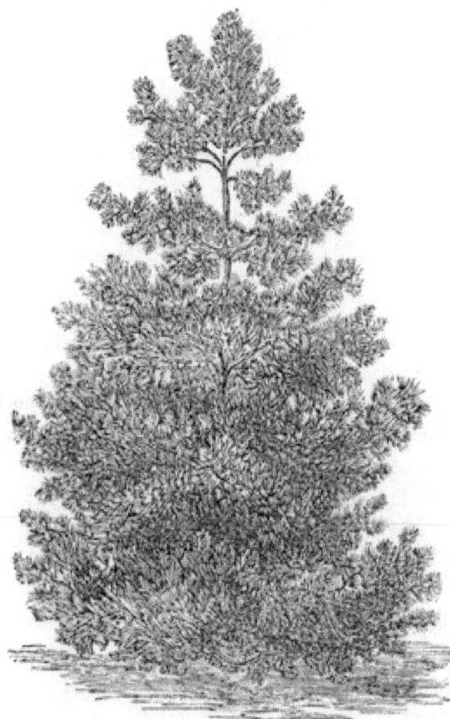

FIG. 31.—THE SCOTCH PINE.

specimens of it in the barren sands of islands in Lake Michigan. Those same plants, however, are now some of them trees forty feet high and extremely beautiful. It has a swayed drooping habit as it grows, but makes a conical and very graceful tree. The foliage is short, light yellowish green, and so unlike any other variety that it is extremely valuable even in grounds of quite limited extent. It is perfectly hardy.

THE SCOTCH PINE. *Pinus sylvestris.*—The Scotch Pine is perhaps one of the most rapid growers among pines, and is also very easy of management, transplanting with rarely a failure, and growing freely in almost any soil or situation. While young, it forms a pretty compact tree; but as it acquires age, the lower limbs sway toward the ground, giving it rather a picturesque than beautiful appearance. The low price at which trees of it have been sold, together with its easy and rapid growth, have induced its planting, until we confess to its having become to us wearisome. It may be sparingly introduced in the formation of groups or masses; and for picturesque distant views, and for belts or masses for breaking the force of storms and wind, it is very desirable; but as a single tree, or for groups in small grounds, we prefer to leave it out.

THE CORSICAN PINE. *Pinus larico.*—The Corsican Pine is a variety between the Scotch and Austrian—with the general habit of growth of the Scotch, perhaps not as much sway to its branches as it grows old — leaves somewhat longer than the Scotch, but not as long or as dark a green as the Austrian, more yellowish. It transplants and grows with the same facility as the Scotch, and is desirable as a variety and to form groups or masses with that or other varieties.

THE BENTHAM PINE. *Pinus Benthamiana.* — The Bentham Pine is comparatively of recent introduction, and where spreading stateliness of character is wanted, either in a single tree or group, that or the Heavy Wooded Pine—*Pinus ponderosa*—promise to supply the object. It is of rapid growth, with dark green foliage, long leaves in tufts, but instead of being compact, it is open, and stately and majestic in form. We should group it with the European sycamore, the tulip or magnolia trees.

THE HEAVY WOODED PINE. *Pinus ponderosa.*—The Ponderous or Heavy Wooded Pine is another variety like the last-named, of comparatively recent introduction. It is also of a stately habit, with long leaves of a rich yellow green color

FIG. 32.—THE PONDEROUS PINE.

This as well as Bentham's Pine attain a very large size when fully grown, and are therefore adapted only to positions where room can be given them in future years. We do not know how well they may bear pinching or rubbing back to reduce their size and increase their compactness, but judging from their habit, doubt the value of such practice with them.

THE CALABRIAN PINE. *Pinus brutia.*—This is an exceedingly rare and very beautiful variety, resembling the Austrian, but with somewhat longer leaves, each of which presents a twisted wavy character, and a shade of green half way between the Corsican and Austrian in color. In its original native land—the mountains of Calabria—it grows to a height of seventy to one

FIG. 33.—CALABRIAN PINE.

hundred feet, and judging from specimens we have seen here, it promises even to surpass its native height. For positions singly upon broad open lawns, or to crown some headland point, it has the characteristics of form, color, and broad majestic stateliness to make its use very effective.

Once it becomes of seed-bearing age, the remarkable massing or clustering of its cones adds greatly to its beauty and attractiveness. Whenever this variety can be procured to take the place in grouping of, or in association with, the Austrian, it should be planted; but at present it is so rare that we can only look for its being placed in some prominent single position upon the lawn.

THE SWISS STONE PINE. *Pinus cembra.*—The Cembrian or Swiss Stone Pine is a very compact and somewhat slow-growing variety, resembling the white pine, except that its foliage is shorter and more stiff. It is well suited to the foreground of groups of that variety. It is perfectly hardy, and very handsome.

THE PITCH PINE. *Pinus rigida.*—For the purpose of creating a wild and somewhat romantic effect upon some rocky hillside, or in the formation of a broken group, the pitch pine may be used with good effect; but as a tree for general use in ornamental planting, the dark rich green of its foliage, and the facility with which it can be grown in any soil, are its only claims to notice.

THE NORWAY PINE. *Pinus resinosa.*—The Red or Norway Pine is of rapid growth, quite handsome while young, its foliage being a dark rich green; but as it acquires age it becomes sometimes too open and sparse of foliage to render it specially desirable, except in large grounds. In the formation of masses we should use one or more of this variety.

THE MAMMOTH TREE OF CALIFORNIA. *Sequoia gigantea.*—The growth and appearance of this new California evergreen is extremely graceful and beautiful. It is known under the various names of *Washingtonia*, *Wellingtonia*, and Bastard Cedar, and was originally classed as a *Taxodium*, supposing it to belong to the same genus as the deciduous cypress. It was first discovered in 1831. It has been found growing abundantly on the mountains of Santa Cruz, about sixty miles from Monterey, in Cali-

fornia, where its average height is two hundred feet, with trunks
from eighteen to twenty-four feet in circumference, quite straight
and clear of branches to the height of sixty or seventy feet.   It
grows rapidly in almost any soil, and may yet become one of
our most valuable timber trees for planting South and West.

The wood is of a beautiful red, fine and close-grained, light
and durable, and like red cedar never attacked by insects.

FIG. 34.—MAMMOTH TREE OF CALIFORNIA.

As an ornamental tree, it must be used where room can be
given, looking forward to its immense ultimate growth.   As a
graceful lawn tree, or as a center tree to an extensive group of
cypress, both evergreen and deciduous, larch, birch, etc., it is
well suited by its strong yet light and airy character.   With

foliage between the arborvitæ and cypress, it throws out its limbs or branches at first horizontally; but they soon assume a gentle graceful curve, that gives to the tree a light, easy, and attractively pleasing form, rendering it very desirable for planting in grounds of considerable extent, or for the bordering of some parts of a wide avenue or entrance road to an estate. Its hardihood is perhaps not yet perfectly tested at the North; but

Fig. 35.—The Lawson Cypress.

from its native habitat, and the many exposures that trees of it have received, and their so far success, there is every reason to believe that it will prove hardy in most locations.

The tree, from the peculiar habit it has of making perpendicular rather than horizontal roots, should be transplanted while quite young, say not more than two or three years old. To insure perfect success, it is best to obtain young plants in pots.

THE THUJOPSIS BOREALIS is a new evergreen, with delicate foliage, resembling somewhat the cypress, rather dark in color, of a rapid growth, hardy; and for planting where delicacy in spray and foliage is desirable, it promises of value. We have seen few specimens of any size.

THE LAWSON CYPRESS. *Cupressus Lawsoniana.*—This we consider one of the greatest acquisitions that has been made for many years to our list of hardy evergreens. Its foliage resembles the arborvitæ, but its habit is that of the hemlock. As a lawn tree, or for association and planting near water, or in cemeteries where there is room, its beauty of foliage and form renders it every way desirable. There is a variety of this called Pyramidalis, that is more dense and upright, but to us not as beautiful.

THE BALSAM FIR. *Picea balsamea.*—The Balsam Fir is a very handsome, compact, erect-pointed tree while young; but as it acquires age its lower limbs die away; and as a single tree it often presents a ragged, neglected appearance. As a center tree, or for points in the formation of groups, it is desirable; and as a tree for belts, where very heavy winds are experienced, it proves admirably adapted. In light, sandy soils its beauty lasts about twelve years, while in rich, deep clay loams it carries its foliage on the lower limbs and its beauty from twenty to thirty years. Where it can be had cheap, it is well suited for massing, using the European Silver Fir and American Spruce for outsides.

THE EUROPEAN SILVER FIR. *Picea pectinata.*—The European Silver Fir is one of our most beautiful evergreen trees. From its slow growth while young, and often losing its leading shoot until it gains a height of six to eight feet, many persons neglect planting it. They, however, do not know its lasting beauty and permanence of form as it acquires age, or they would never leave it out of a collection. Its branches are spreading horizontally erect, while its foliage is always a rich dark green on the upper side, and silvery underneath, and, unlike many other evergreens, it never looks dingy at any season of the year. A rich, deep, rather moist soil suits it best, and it groups elegantly with magnolia acuminata, the American ash, and ginko. It does not

FIG. 36.—THE EUROPEAN SILVER FIR.

answer well as a screen plant for belts, being unable to endure exposed situations where severe winds and storms beat against it, and yet it is perfectly hardy. It should be remembered, when planting, that this tree acquires a large size, and must have plenty of room.

THE NORDMAN'S FIR. *Picea Nordmaniana.*—This is an old
variety, but comparatively rare. It is of rapid growth, with
rich green foliage, that attracts attention at once. It is perfectly hardy, and should be more generally grown and planted.

THE PINSAPO FIR. *Picea Pinsapo.*—This is an elegant tree,
with short, roundish, sharp-pointed leaves, set thick around all

FIG. 37.—THE AMERICAN WHITE SPRUCE.

its branches and shoots, giving the tree rather a stiff, but unique
and beautiful appearance. It is quite hardy, and so distinct and
regular as to make it desirable as a lawn or single tree. The
Noble Silver Fir, the Mount Enos Fir, Hudson's Bay Fir, and

Cephalonian Fir are all hardy, and varieties of value in large grounds. The Cephalonian is of a spreading habit, broad rather than high, and for planting in position where some ground scene is desirable to be hidden without obstructing the upper view, is a tree for adoption.

THE AMERICAN WHITE SPRUCE. *Abies alba.*—For planting in small grounds, for the outskirts of groups and masses, for points on roadways, and for cemeteries, the American White and Red Spruces are deserving of far more general use than they have received. Pyramidal tapering, regular and yet irregular, compact without losing its pleasing variety of regular outline, attaining only a moderate size, the White Spruce is far more suited to position on small lawns or outside masses, or borders of half-acre lots, than the Norway, which is much more commonly planted.

THE AMERICAN RED SPRUCE. *Abies rubra.*—The American Red Spruce has a half drooping habit, especially of its young branches, and its whole form while rising to a cone is decidedly picturesque. As a tree to aid in creating a romantic effect on a rocky point, or to associate with the flowing ease and mellowness of water scenery, it is well suited; and so also from its limited size and irregular drooping yet airy form, counterbalanced by its dark and almost gloomy foliage, is it well adapted for planting in cemeteries.

THE NORWAY SPRUCE. *Abies excelsa.*—The Norway Spruce is now *the* popular evergreen tree for all planting. Unfortunately, it is used without regard to appropriateness of position or space, and hence, while beautiful in itself when allowed room for development, it frequently has to be so mutilated, in order to keep it within the limit which can be granted, that it is no more a Norway Spruce, or tree of beauty. Of the thousands sold and planted, few, comparatively, ever exhibit the character of grandeur and graceful beauty that belongs to the true Norway.

4

Among the millions in nurseries, all grown from seed, a large number have no characteristics to ever make them trees of grandeur, while yet they may be trees of beauty. The planter in selecting should look for plants with long, pendent shoots, rather than stiff, erect, or horizontal ones, as it is only the former

FIG. 38.—THE AMERICAN RED SPRUCE.

that will make trees of the greatest beauty. For masses or groups, this swaying, drooping, picturesquely-graceful habit is of less consequence than when the tree is to stand by itself, and for hedge or belt screen growing, to which the Norway is well adapted, the close, stiff, erect-growing plants are probably the best. The Norway bears the shears with impunity, but, except for hedges, or perhaps the shortening of an occasional irregularly extending branch, we consider the use of shears as a practice in clipping the trees as erroneous, and creating only a stiff

FIG. 33.—THE NORWAY SPRUCE.

bank or cone of green where there should be flowing lines and light and shade, varying with every breeze. The Norway does the best in a light, rich loam, but will grow freely in any soil not wet. In positions where it develops itself fully as a single tree, or for grouping or massing, it is one of the very finest; but the planter who can give to it only an area of ten to fifteen feet diameter should substitute the American White Spruce in its place.

As we have said, there are in the seed rows of growers many varieties, some of which are occasionally selected out and spe-

FIG. 40.—THE HEMLOCK SPRUCE.

cifically named, and the experienced amateur or professional man can select from them trees to make a great diversity of form, habit of growth, and shade of foliage, by which he will add to the beauty of a park or small private grounds, and yet have all Norway Spruces.

THE HEMLOCK SPRUCE. *Abies Canadensis.*—The hemlock, common in all portions of our Union, possesses features of elegance and beauty unlike that of any other hardy variety. When standing alone, or on the outskirts of small groups, its dark yet loose-looking foliage, hanging in pendulous tufts from its peculiarly graceful, half-curving branches, renders the tree one of the most ornamental, and suited to a place in decorating the grounds of almost every residence. It is a tree that bears the shears well, and is therefore adapted to hedge or screen planting. When grown in the nursery, it is no more difficult to transplant than other evergreens, although it has been declared very sensitive of removal—probably by those who had no experience except with its removal from the woods. It is, as we have said, a beautiful tree for the open lawn, but it lacks stateliness to adapt it for position near the main residence or buildings.

ARBOR VITÆ. *Thuja.*—The American arbor vitæ—*thuja occidentalis*—frequently, and perhaps more generally, called white cedar, is one of our most valuable evergreens. Of a regular formal outline in its growth, from the young plant to the tree, it can rarely be used in grouping; but as a single point tree, or for screen belts and hedges, it is one of the most desirable. It may be grown to form a perfect wall or screen thirty or forty feet high, and yet not spread at the base over four or five feet broad. It is easily grown, and as it frequently throws out roots from the stem and branches when covered with earth, in transplanting it is well to set it somewhat deeper than where it has previously been grown.

Of the varieties, a new one under the name of Hovey is probably the most compact, and of the best color; but the Siberian is a valuable one, growing very compact, and keeping its color well in the winter season. *Thuja ericoides* is of a more delicate foliage; sometimes browns badly in the winter, where fully exposed to the sun; while the Tom Thumb, sent out by Messrs.

Ellwanger & Barry, is a very dwarf compact sort, especially adapted as a point plant on beds or divisions of pathways. All the above, as well as the Chinese and the variegated-foliaged varieties, are adapted for planting as single trees; and as they bear the knife perfectly, may be kept clipped and pruned into any shape or form desired to harmonize with their position. The American, however, is the one most generally used in the planting for hedges and screens; not that it is any better than the Siberian or some others, for it is not naturally as compact, but because it is a rapid grower, and can be obtained at a less cost than other varieties. In setting it for hedges, where it is designed to keep the plants clipped to a height never exceeding four to six feet, the plants should stand one in a foot of length in the row; but where it is designed to form screens or belts, growing twenty to forty feet high, one plant in four feet is sufficient. Any good soil suits the arbor vitæ, and it bears water or wet grounds even better than dry.

As an avenue tree for the north and west sides of driveways that are to be used in winter, it is one the best suited, and every country place should have one or more pathways sheltered by it for resort in a clear winter's day when the sun is shining brightly, and at the same time a cold north wind prevailing.

RED CEDAR. *Juniperus.*—The red cedar of our country— *juniperus Virginiana*—is only occasionally planted, because of its generally rather stiff habit, and dull dingy brown color of foliage in winter and spring. There are, however, among the many plants grown from seed, varieties that have more or less of a drooping and graceful form, and whose color keeps a clear light blue green, making their association or connection with other evergreens often very harmonious and agreeable.

In poor, dry, rocky soils the red cedar thrives finely, and it seems equally at home in rich, deep loams. It does not answer well for hedges, as clipped plants after twelve or more years are liable to become open, ragged, and unsightly. In some sections we have seen roadsides planted with the red cedar, but their appearance is not that of beauty or grandeur, and its use for such purpose can not be commended.

With the English juniper—*communis*—there is a classical association which we have occasionally heard strained to that of the red cedar, as the tree mentioned in Holy Writ under which the prophet Elijah took refuge in the wilderness of Beersheba to avoid the persecutions of King Ahab.

LEBANON CEDAR. *Cedrus Libani.*—The cedar of Lebanon, Indian or Deodar cedar, African or silver cedar, Japan cedar, and some others, are all beautiful trees; but in the Northern and Middle States they are not perfectly hardy, and therefore can not be recommended for general planting. Where, however, they endure the climate, their beauty of foliage, the stateliness and wide-spreading habits of the Lebanon and silver cedars, the pendulous graceful habit of the Indian and Japan cedars, should not be forgotten by the planter, but their free use made a point to the exclusion of many sorts more common and of less historical association.

As lawn trees, the light, airy, graceful characters of the Japan and Deodar cedars render them specially beautiful, and as we have said, wherever the climate is such that they can be grown safely, their planting should not be omitted.

CHAPTER VI.

WEEPING EVERGREEN TREES.

THE number of hardy evergreen trees that possess distinct drooping habits to class them among weeping trees is very limited. Unfortunately the funebral cypress, introduced some twelve or fifteen years since, and from which so much was

FIG. 41.—WEEPING JUNIPER.

hoped on account of coming from the north of China, has proved tender in all exposed situations throughout the Northern and Middle States. Of the few on which reliance can be placed, the *juniperus oblonga pendula* is of a small growth, making a plant often not more than eight to twelve feet high, but with horizontal branches from which drooping spray depends in an irregular fastigiate manner, creating for it a charm and picturesqueness that together with its size make it one of the most desirable plants for position in cemeteries. In small grounds, or for special positions in ornamental planting, it is also extremely pretty, but should be used with great care and thought in studying association with the surrounding plants and trees.

Juniperus Virginiana pendula is of a stronger and more vigorous habit, sending up a strong center stem with recurved horizontal drooping branches, highly picturesque and adapted to rocky or water scenery.

Thuja filiformis is a variety of the arbor vitæ, with horizontal branches and long depending twigs or spray, giving a unique and pleasing form, that with its light, yellowish green shade of foliage is always attractive and interesting rather than beautiful.

It is well suited for cemetery purposes, and may occasionally be introduced near ponds or pools of water.

4*

CHAPTER VII.

EVERGREEN SHRUBS.

A MORE common, free, and abundant use of evergreen shrubs should be adopted, because of the cheerful, bright, verdure-like appearance produced in the landscape when their dark and light green foliage and blue or scarlet berries cover with harmonious life-like beauty what otherwise in the dreary winter scenes would be barren and unsightly. Their use among deciduous shrubs can be more general than that of evergreen trees, from the fact that they only rise a few feet, and therefore, unlike trees, can not exhibit shade and gloom to the scene. Many a place is made beautiful in summer from the foliage of shrubs and the bloom of flowers, that in winter presents a dreary barren aspect, which is easily changed and draped with foliage and beauty by the simple planting of evergreen shrubs. Were we to write an entire book in advocating their general use, it would not half express our feelings, or perhaps any more advance their frequent planting than our present few words. To the planter who seeks to create constant beauty, or who desires easy gradations and harmonious combinations in landscape; to him who has but small grounds in the suburbs of a city; to those who desire to clothe the last resting-place of earthly friends with emblems of eternity and lasting beauty, let me urge upon their attention the claims found in, and beauty derived from, the use of shrub evergreens.

Among the most hardy, and adapted to all sections and positions, the JUNIPER in its varieties is, perhaps, most worthy of frequent and universal planting. There is, as we have described, trees under this head that do not bear clipping; but all the dwarf or naturally small-sized trees of this class bear well a free use of the shears, and may be kept in any form or shape agreeable to the wants or taste of man.

The Swedish juniper—*suecica*—is of a pyramidal habit, with a bluish green foliage and quite rapid growth. It sometimes is liable to break down from our winter snows or severe storms, and should therefore have a wrapping of small wires to keep it in form. Its growth is from ten to twenty feet high, although it may be kept, by means of clipping, down to a height of only five to eight feet. It is adapted to point groups on the corners

FIG. 42.—IRISH JUNIPER AND SAVIN.

of diverging roadways or paths, and with the podocarpus and Irish juniper very effective little clusters may be formed.

The Irish juniper—*Hibernica*—forms one of the prettiest of little point trees; it is perfectly hardy, and always keeps a beautiful rich green color, rather darker than the Swedish. It can be kept at any height, from that of two feet upward to five or six. The common juniper—*communis* var. *Canadensis*—is well known, but too rarely planted because it is common. Singly, upon a lawn, it grows rapidly; and although rising but a few feet high, it spreads over a broad surface and forms a remarkable and effective object. *Juniperus squamata* is also a variety effective as a large spreading plant upon an extensive lawn. *Juniperus nana* and *echiniformis* are of a lighter, more yellow green and compact habit, and for positions where only a limited space can be given them, are very beautiful. They are nearer allied to the *juniperus sabina*, or common savin, a variety well known, and that forms one of the best masses of low growth among the whole collection.

The *juniperus prostrata* is a very low creeping variety, of value in rock-work, and for massing and forming a low evergreen bed upon a lawn. It is admirable also for planting on small mounds and in cemeteries over the graves of the departed.

FIG. 43.—COMMON JUNIPER AND PROSTRATE JUNIPER.

There are many more varieties, but as yet comparatively scarce; all, however, or nearly all, promise to prove hardy and of value in forming features of beauty in a landscape. We have seen a most beautiful mass made of junipers by taking the Swedish as the center plants, then the canadensis circling it, and intermingling the squamata and sabina with here and there a hibernica, and toning down with nana, to an outside finish with prostrata.

DWARF PINES.—There are several varieties of the pine family

that are extremely valuable in the formation of groups and masses of low evergreens, among them one under name of *pinus pumilio*, or dwarf mountain pine, is most commonly in use. It is classed by many as identical with *pinus pumilio mughus*, or mugho pine, but the specimens we have had to deal with under the latter name have been of a more compact and diminutive growth, although the leaf and color are similar.

For positions where a compact, round-headed plant from six to twelve feet high is wanted, and for forming a foreground to large masses of round-headed pines, or for use in small yards, the dwarf mountain pine is exceedingly valuable. It is perfectly hardy, of a deep rich green color, and when grown by itself, fully exposed, it forms a very compact small tree. In small pieces of rock-work, and for crowning slight elevations at the turn of roads, etc., we have found its use very effective.

BROAD-LEAVED YEW — *Podocarpus.*—The broad-leaved or long-leaved Japan yew is not hardy in all parts of the Northern and Middle States when fully exposed; but there are many locations in almost every place of any considerable extent where groups of shrub evergreens are wanted, and where considerable shelter may be afforded; in all such, and in some sections, as around New York, southern New Jersey, and on south and west, it is a very desirable variety to plant. The tree is erect, compact, with a rich dark green broad leaf, distinct and beautiful. There are a number of varieties, but the *japonica* and *taxifolia* are probably the hardiest. Any good loamy soil suits it.

YEW TREE — *Taxus.*—All of the yew family are beautiful plants, and of great value in making up a place. When fully exposed to the sun, they sometimes burn and brown in winter; but wherever they are shaded by having a position on the north side of buildings, the northern slope of a hill, or the north side of a group of large evergreens, they retain their color per-

fcetly. The common English yew—*baccata*—is the one most
generally grown. It forms a bush of from six to twelve feet
high, and when old enough to fruit, forms one of the most
elegant of evergreen shrubs.

The *erecta* is more compact and upright, not as spreading, in
its habit; while the *horizontalis* is spreading, almost creeping,
in its growth. There are also several varieties with variegated
foliage very curious and ornamental. The Irish yew—*Hibernica*—

FIG. 44.—ASH BERBERRY.

is of slow, compact, upright growth, forming a very small,
round, pillar-like tree, but it will not endure any exposure to
the winter suns. The American yew—*Canadensis*—is, perhaps,
the most hardy of all, but it is not of as rich and dark a green.
As a class, however, masses of them are very beautiful; and when
azaleas are mingled with them the result is quite satisfactory,
especially in spring, when the azaleas are in bloom. In England,

the yew is used more or less for hedges; but as a hedge plant, except in positions shaded from the mid-day sun, and for the purpose of variety, its use in this country is not advisable.

ASH BERBERRY—*Mahonia.*—Among all the shrub evergreens, the mahonia for general use is, without exception, one of the most valuable. In general appearance of leaf it much resembles the European holly, a plant that is not hardy in the Northern or Middle States; it is of the easiest possible culture, growing freely in any soil not wet. Besides its glossy foliage, in spring it gives a profusion of bright yellow flowers, followed with rich purple berries, making it ever attractive and ornamentally beautiful. Our drawing represents a bush of the variety *aquifolium,* with a cluster of flowers. This is the most common sort, and is, perhaps, the best for masses or low hedges; but where a single plant only is to be grown, we should select the *fascicularis* as being more unique in form of foliage, and more subdued in the tone of color. In fully exposed positions facing south, the mahonia occasionally browns and loses its foliage; but we have never known the plants to kill, and early in spring it puts on new leaves and comes forward rapidly, blooming as if it had suffered no loss.

BOX TREE—*Buxus.*—The common dwarf box—*buxus suffruticosa*—is well known, for it is, perhaps, the very best dwarf edging plant for flower-beds and borders that is known. It should always be transplanted early in the spring, and, by a clipping with shears from year to year, never permitted to grow above six to eight inches in height. The tree box—*buxus sempervirens*—forms a pretty dwarf ornamental tree for decorating small lawns or grass-plots, or for rounded points of pathways, etc. There are several varieties among them, comprising *latifolia,* or broad-leaved, which is the best; the *mystifolia,* very narrow-leaved; the *aurea,* or golden variegated-leaved; the *argentea,* or silvery variegated-leaved. A sandy or light gravelly soil seems best to suit the wants of the box tree, and a partial shade from southern suns is requisite to enable it to retain its foliage.

EVERGREEN THORN—*Pyracantha.*—The fiery or evergreen thorn—*cratægus pyracantha*—is an evergreen shrub, at present only to be found occasionally in some amateur's grounds, but highly deserving a place everywhere that ornament or beauty is sought to be created.

As a single plant, it has rare attractive features in its clusters

FIG. 45.—EVERGREEN THORN.

of white flowers, blooming in the month of May, followed by round brilliant scarlet berries, that often remain on a great part of winter, and from whence its name of fiery thorn. In forming low-growing hedges, it is one of the very best plants, as it is perfectly hardy, and bears the shears as well as other thorns. Our engraving shows a plant with a few clusters of flowers. Any good rich garden soil will answer to grow it.

COTONEASTER.—The cotoneaster is a family of plants that for

rock-work and positions where they were not exposed to the south, we have found in use very attractive and effective.

There are three or four varieties, all with white flowers, and all of a low, rather pendant and creeping habit, and their use should be more generally adopted, especially in rock-work, or as undergrowth in shaded situations.

ANDROMEDA.—Two varieties of andromeda, viz.: *floribunda* and *polifolia*, are described by Mr. Fuller in his "Forest Tree Culturist" as worthy of extensive cultivation. They are of slow growth, with lanceolate leaves and white flowers, forming pretty,

FIG. 46.—KALMIA.

low shrubs, and suited even to wet soils. We have had no experience with them.

EUONYMUS OR SPINDLE TREE.—This is a class of beautiful evergreen shrubs that prove partially hardy about New York, and are suited for planting in the Southern States; but they can not be depended upon anywhere north.

HOLLY—*Ilex.*—The European holly is so beautiful in England, that almost every planter of a new place feels anxious to adopt it. Repeated experiments with it, however, compel us to, all unwillingly, write that it can not be used and prove at all satisfactory. Even our native variety, the *ilex opaca*, frequently browns badly, and occasionally loses its foliage completely; and although beautiful when it can be perfectly grown, it proves so often unsightly rather than beautiful, that it is unwise to use it except in shaded situations.

MOUNTAIN LAUREL—*Kalmia.*—The kalmia, or laurel as it is commonly called, is one of the finest evergreen under shrubs. It is perfectly hardy in any exposure, but it chooses a soil largely composed of vegetable loam and sand. Near running water it grows and blooms most freely, but naturally it is found often in the most barren rocky situations imaginable. As an under shrub it is particularly desirable, as it bears the drip of other trees without perceptible injury. Its flowers are produced most freely in June, but it continues more or less of bloom for a month or six weeks in succession. The *latifolia*, see engraving, and *augustifolia* and narrow-leaved, or sheep laurel, are the most valued varieties. The flowers of the former are a white or light pink delicately spotted, while those of the sheep laurel are dark red.

RHODODENDRON.—The rhododendrons, or rose bay as sometimes called, are a class of broad-leaved evergreen shrubs of exceeding beauty both in foliage and flower. Like the kalmia, they succeed best when grown in soil composed mostly of vegetable loam and sand, although some cultivators advise free use of well-rotted animal manures. Such application we have found to produce free growth, but at expense of hardihood, and when necessary to improve the soil, advise fresh woods loam rather than animal manure. The varieties *maximum* and *catawbiense* have been tested as to hardihood all over the Union, and everywhere proved successful. Many others are probably equally hardy when grown under the same circumstances; but a large proportion of those sold from year to year are imported plants, and in getting acclimated, too often die. We consider the great secret in growing rhododendrons successfully, consists in keeping the soil *cool* and *moist*, and this is best done by surface dressing of light half-decayed leaves a depth of three or four inches over the soil in which the roots are growing.

A free use in planting of kalmias and rhododendrons in the

FIG. 47.—RHODODENDRON.

small yards and gardens of our suburban residences would give to them a cheerful living brightness in winter, and add largely to their beauty at all seasons.

CNEORUM—*Daphne.*—The garland flower, or trailing *Daphne cneorum*, has been only recently introduced to notice, although an old and well-known plant. For rock-work planting, for points on beds or borders, it is one of the best as well as attractive plants. Its flowers are bright pink, sweet scented, and produced freely in April and May, and again in September.

CHAPTER VIII.

ORNAMENTAL DECIDUOUS SHRUBS.

In all grounds a well-appointed and arranged shrubbery is a most effective and cheerful feature; and in grounds of small extent, such as the front gardens of suburban city lots, the use of shrubs or trees of small growth is more to be commended than those of a towering or large spreading habit. Just enough of large trees should be planted to form necessary shade, and then the effect and general impression of beauty be created by the planting of deciduous and evergreen shrubs. One of the most important things in planting shrubs is to attend particularly to the shades of green in foliage; another is, an understanding of the soils and situation in which they will grow and develop themselves most luxuriantly. "Flowers continue but for a short period in comparison with the duration of the leaves, and therefore the more permanent picture should be executed by judiciously contrasting the green. Even the effect of perspective may be considerably increased by the proper arrangement of hues. Shrubs whose leaves are of a gray or bluish tint, when seen over or between shrubs of a yellowish or bright green, will seem thrown into the distance. Those, again, with small or tremulous leaves, should wave over or before those with large, broad-fixed foliage. Where the situation will permit, three or five lilacs may be grouped together in one place, or as many laburnums in another, so as to give effect in various parts by a mass of color."

"A shrubbery," says Mr. Phillips, "should be planted as a court or stage dress is ornamented, for general effect, and not for particular and partial inspection. Boldness of design, which seems to be more the offspring of nature and chance than of art and study, should be attempted; but though boldness is what the planter should aspire to, all harshness or too great abruptness must be avoided by a judicious mixture of plants whose colors will blend easily with one another." The most beautiful shrubs should of course be planted in the most conspicuous places, and the whole with respect to evergreens so arranged as to contribute in making bright the gloom of winter; in reducing and softening the glare of summer, and assist in lengthening the season by their early flowers in spring and their ripening berries in autumn.

The ACACIA—*Robinia*.—The rose acacia (*Robinia hispida*) is an old shrub commonly well known, but latterly little planted. Its large clusters of rose-colored flowers in July are extremely beautiful, and as it commences flowering when only some two feet high, rarely rising above four or five feet, there are many places where its introduction in the foreground is productive of pleasing effects. The objection to it has been its tendency to throw up numerous suckers from its long, straggling roots; but these may easily be kept in bounds by regular cutting back with a sharp spade in August. It can be grafted on the stronger-growing varieties of the locust, when it forms a small, very pretty, and ornamental round head, quite well suited to position on some small lawns.

The CLAMMY BARKED LOCUST—*Robinia viscosa*—grows to a height of ten or fifteen feet, and has a gummy substance over its branches that makes it unpleasant to the touch. It has large pale pink flowers, and in forming large clusters of shrubs and second-class trees it is often desirable. There are a number of other varieties, such as *inermis, tortuosa, grandiflora*, etc., all more or less beautiful when placed in large groups, but not of themselves sufficiently ornamental for single positions in small grounds. In rock-work planting, the *hispida* may be used advantageously.

The ALTHEA—*Hibiscus Syriacus.*—The rose of Sharon, as it is most commonly called, is a shrub of almost universal use in planting. It grows from six to eight feet high, and does best in light dry soils. It is of a stiff, formal shape, even when left to take its own natural way; but as it bears the shears well, and in fact seems thereby to increase its blooms, plants may be so clipped as to present broad masses of foliage and flowers from the ground upward. As an ornamental hedge plant it takes on its foliage too late in spring, and is also partially tender, occasionally killing during a very cold winter. There are varieties with white pink or purple and variegated flowers, both single and double. It blooms during the last of August or early in September, and where single plants are wanted of a regular systematic form, or for the back-plants of masses on straight lines, it is valuable.

The ALDER—*Alnus.*—Until within a few years the alder has not been much planted, but recently there have been introduced some varieties with foliage so strikingly marked, that wherever there is a moist soil, or a low group is wanted near a spring, their planting will be found advisable.

Of the varieties most prized are the oak-leaved, the serrate-leaved, and the lasciniated or cut-leaved. In growth, the alder usually rises to a height of about ten to twenty feet, with foliage all of a dark green color.

The ALMOND—*Amygdalus.*—The dwarf double flowering almond—*amygdalus pumila*—is one of the oldest flowering shrubs of our knowledge. Its period of early flowering (April), together with their profusion and beauty; its slender twigs and general graceful delicacy in form of growth; the perfect hardihood of the plant, all combine to make it a shrub of great value in decorative gardening. On account of its low growth and

delicacy of stem, it should always be planted in the foreground
of a group or upon the point of a pathway, where it can display
its beautiful formed flowers, like little roses, in the most conspicuous manner. There is a rose-colored and white-flowered
variety, both equally free bloomers. The white is especially
desirable for planting in cemeteries, and masses well with
mahonias.

The AZALEA.—The azaleas *nudiflora* and *viscosa* are, we
believe, the varieties most common to this country. They are
found wild in many parts of the Northern and Middle States,

FIG. 48.—AZALEA.

and are generally known as swamp pink or swamp honeysuckle.
They are perfectly hardy, and the beauty and fragrance of their
flowers when in bloom render them plants of rare value and
interest in forming masses or groups of shrubs, and especially
for mingling with rhododendrons and other small evergreens.
The *pontica*, we believe, is the only foreign variety proved to be
perfectly hardy; but there are a great many of the Belgian
varieties that may be grown with little trouble in tubs or pots,

kept in a pit frame during winter, and placed in the out-door shrubbery on approach of spring. The flowers produced in May of our native varieties are almost white, varying to a pink, while those of the *pontica* are a bright yellow. Writers say they must have peat soil in order to succeed, but we have found any good loamy soil to answer, provided we mulched it with leaves or leaf mold. The same soil and care suitable for growing rhododendrons answers well for azaleas.

The AMORPHA.—There are a number of varieties of the amorpha or bastard indigo, all more or less ornamental, both from their foliage as well as their long spikes of blue or purple flowers produced in July and August. Their stems occasionally die after three or more years old, hence they should always be grown in the bush form, cutting out the oldest stems from year to year. Any good garden soil will answer for them, provided it is not too wet or too dry.

The variety *nana* is the most dwarf, growing only one to two feet high; *glabra*, growing four to six feet; and *fragrans*, eight or more feet in height. They are all good for planting on the borders of water-streams or ponds, and also for strong contrasts and backgrounds in masses.

The AMELANCHIER.—Under the common name of shad bush, the *amelanchier vulgaris* is well known and admired, when in early spring its peculiarly-formed flowers cover the tree, as it were, like a white sheet. It is then seen at a distance as beautiful as any of the magnolias, and when planted so that some evergreen shall be contiguous and form its background, no plant creates more universal attention or admiration. It makes a small tree of from twelve to twenty feet high.

The JUNE BERRY—*A. botryapium*—has also white flowers in April, hanging in pendulous racemes; the bark and wood more smooth, and the tree of not quite as large growth as the shad bush. It is a very desirable small tree for door-yards or small confined situations, and its blossoms are followed by fruit often very palatable in the month of June.

There is also a variety of this with the young wood of a dark red or blood color, but its flowers and fruit are less abundant. Any good soil not wet suits them.

The BERBERRY—*Berberis.*—There are quite a number of varieties of the barberry, all pleasing, ornamental shrubs growing from four to ten feet high, but bearing the shears so well that they may be kept at just any height desired. Massed in a group composed of the varieties, and planting the purple-leaved as the center or background, and interspersing occasionally the variegated-leaved, a good effect is produced without the aid of other shrubs. In spring, or the month of May, their flowers are yellow or deep orange, borne in pendant racemes, followed by bright scarlet or purple fruit, which if left will hang on nearly or quite all winter. As a fancy screen hedge the barberry answers admirably, and a pretty effect is created by interspersing along the row an occasional plant of the purple-leaved, variegated-leaved, etc. A rich deep loam is best fitted for the barberry, but it will grow anywhere if the soil is not wet.

The BUCKTHORN—*Rhamnus.*—As a hedge plant, the buckthorn—*rhamnus catharticus*—has no superior, if indeed it has an equal. The plant is perfectly hardy; never suckers; roots extend but a little distance, and being of fibrous nature do not interfere with the growing of anything even to within a foot of the hedge. It grows in any soil, and no animal, unless it is the goat, feeds upon its leaves; nor is it attacked by insects. Its foliage is of a dark rich green, put on early in spring and retained late in autumn. As an ornamental plant for large groups, or even planted singly, it is very desirable from the habit it can be made to take; the dark rich green of its leaf, the white clusters of flowers in spring, and the dark blue fruit of autumn often hanging into winter. Besides the common

5

variety, there is a broad-leaved sort—*latifolia*—that for single positions is especially attractive from its crimped-like foliage and erect habit.

The BUFFALO TREE—*Sheperdia.*—The peculiar silvery leaves of the *Sheperdia argentea*, or buffalo berry tree as it is commonly called, make it very desirable in grouping, as a foreground to trees or shrubs of darker greens. It bears the shears well, and may be kept at any desired low height, although when left to itself it makes a tree or shrub from ten to fifteen feet high. Its flowers are yellow, and although not particularly beautiful of themselves, yet they are so abundant upon the branches as to make the tree attractive at that season; and in autumn it is very showy from its masses of red or bright scarlet fruit, of size about like currants. The fruit is very valuable for tarts, and aside from its ornamental character renders the shrub one of value for all grounds.

The BLADDER SENNA—*Colutea.*—This is a very attractive shrub; one variety having light yellow flowers, another those of orange color dotted with red, designated as Pocock's senna and *cruenta*, with reddish flowers. It commences blooming in June, and frequently continues many weeks; but its peculiar attraction comes from the delicate light green of its foliage, and the bladder or balloon-like pods that follow its flowers. Its height is usually four to six feet, but it may be kept down by use of the shears in spring.

The BLADDER NUT—*Staphylea.*—The bladder nut—*staphylea trifolia*—is a very pretty shrub or low tree, with light green foliage, and a profusion of small, white bell-shaped flowers in May and early June. It has, however, a disposition to sucker so much, that it is not best to plant it except where there will be little or no stirring of the soil.

The CLETHRA.—Although a native shrub, found in some of its varieties in the low grounds of most sections of the States, the clethra is nevertheless deserving, on account of its beautiful and numerous spikes of white flowers, a place in every collection. All are perfectly hardy, and with exception of the *acuminata*, make shrubs of height. from four to five feet, and blooming

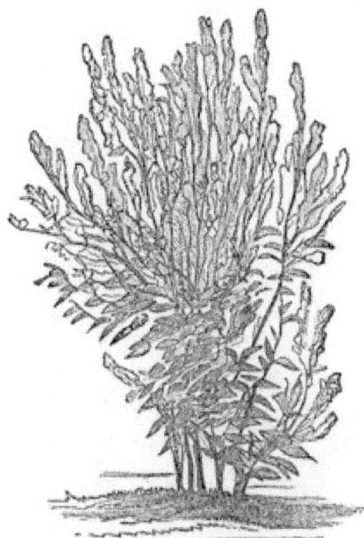

FIG. 49.—CLETHRA.

freely from July to September. The *alnifolia* is most common, and perhaps the best of the varieties. It succeeds well in any good garden soil.

The CURRANT—*Ribes.*—There are a number of very attractive shrubs designated as flowering currants, to distinguish them from varieties grown particularly for their fruit. All are more or less ornamental, and can be grown in almost any soil or situation.

The crimson flowering variety—*sanguineum*—is partially

tender, and can not be relied upon unless protected in winter;
but the *Gordoni*, or Gordon's flowering currant, is perfectly
hardy, a strong, vigorous grower, with long, pendant racemes of
crimson and yellow flowers in May, rendering its appearance
highly attractive and pleasing. It should be in all collections.
The double-flowering crimson—*sanguineum flore pleno*—like its
parent, is partially tender; all the others are hardy. Very pretty

FIG. 50.—GORDON'S CURRANT.

groups or masses for spring show can be made by using the different varieties of flowering currants.

The DEUTZIA.—For foregrounds to masses of shrubbery, or
for producing a profusion of white flowers, the different varieties
of Deutzia have claims to pre-eminence. They are all perfectly
hardy and easily grown in any soil. The rough-leaved or
scabra is the strongest grower, making a shrub from four to five
feet high, with flowers resembling orange blossoms. *Corymbosum*

comes next in growth, then *crenate-leaved*, while *gracilis* is quite a dwarf, say from one to two feet in height.

The ELDER—*Sambucus.*—Although a common wild shrub, the broad cymes of delicate white flowers followed by dark purple or reddish fruit produced on the elder, render it desirable for planting in all large groups of shrubs; and for use in making bouquets, one or more plants of it should be in every collection. There are quite a number of varieties; some with white fruit, others of a reddish tinge; some growing into small trees with single trunks, others forming clusters of stems; some with variegated foliage, and one with a leaf lasciniated so as to be termed parsley leaf. All are of easy cultivation in good deep rich soils.

The GOLDEN BELL SHRUB—*Forsythia.*—The *Forsythia viridissima*, although comparatively of recent introduction, is so easily grown that it has become quite common. It is not perfectly hardy in all locations, but generally succeeds when planted so that it will be shaded from midday or afternoon sun. Its flowers are bright yellow, bell-shaped, produced very early in spring on spurs or wood of two years old or more, and gives most effect when seen against an evergreen as a background. The young wood is a bright greenish yellow; foliage bright lively green, and in shaded positions often retained until Christmas.

The HAWTHORN—*Cratægus.*—In England the *cratægus oxycantha* is largely used as a hedge plant; but trials of it in this country prove it not well suited to endure, when clipped, our strong hot suns and frequent dry seasons. As an ornamental plant, where large groups or masses are to be formed, the beauty of some varieties with their double white, pink, or scarlet flowers in May, render their planting almost a necessity. Left to themselves when planted alone, as is sometimes done on lawns, they form very regular round-headed little trees of ten to fifteen feet high. All may be budded or grafted, and the numerous varieties with varied foliage as well as flowers, render the plan of grafting two or more of a kind on the same stem a very desirable one, especially in small grounds where only room can be given for a few plants.

The HORSE-CHESTNUT—*Pavia.*—The dwarf horse-chestnut—*pavia macrostachya*—is one of the finest low-growing shrubs. There are two varieties, one with white and one with variegated or red flowers, both forming spikes large and showy in July and August. The plants form bushes as it were, often spreading

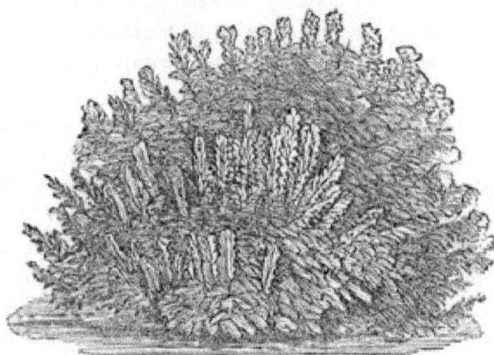

FIG. 51.—DWARF HORSE-CHESTNUT.

many feet wide, but seldom rising above four to six feet in height.

The HOP TREE—*Ptelea.*—A few years since the *ptelea trifoliata* or trefoil tree acquired a general although transient reputation as a plant to grow for the value of its seed capsules, as substitutes for hops, and under the name of hop tree thousands were sold. As an ornamental low tree when trained to a single stem it is very pretty and desirable for planting in the foreground of groups.

The HYDRANGEA.—Most of the hydrangeas require protection

during the winters at the North; but there are some varieties, as the oak-leaved—*quercifolia*, heart-leaved—*cordata*, and some others, that prove hardy; and for positions where low-growing plants with large foliage are required, they are particularly well adapted, and from their large spikes of greenish white flowers measurably ornamental. Hydrangea *Deutziafolia* is a new variety of good promise, and should be tested.

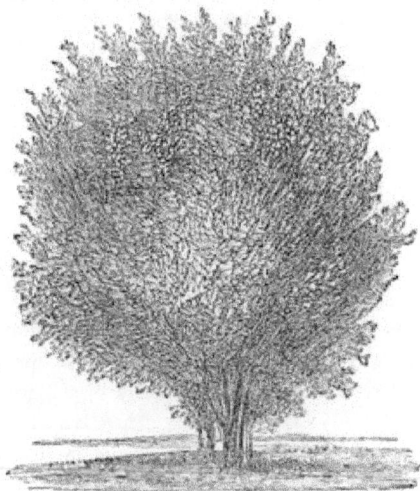

FIG. 52.—UPRIGHT OR TREE HONEYSUCKLE.

The UPRIGHT HONEYSUCKLE—*Lonicera*.—The tree or Tartarian honeysuckles are hardy and beautiful shrubs, blooming early in June. In foliage they are quite handsome, and the flower being followed with fruit makes them desirable in all grounds, even of the smallest. They grow freely in all soils, attaining, if left unclipped, a height of ten or twelve feet; but they should be annually clipped and kept down to four or five feet. Very pretty ornamental hedges can be formed by mingling the different colored flowering sorts. The *rubra*, *alba*, and *pulve-rulenta* are among, if not the best.

The HIPPOPHAE.—This is a low-growing shrub with narrow leaves, downy whitish underneath, of no great beauty, but pleasing and desirable as a foreground plant in forming large masses. Some of the varieties have been described as growing to a height of fifteen or more feet; but we have never seen any above six feet, and oftener as low bushes of two or three feet. Its flowers are of a bright yellow, and its blooms in May are followed with orange-colored fruit that often hangs on all winter, rendering the effect when massed with evergreens very good.

The JAPAN GLOBE FLOWER.—The Japan globe flower—*Kerria Japonica*—but a few years since was universally planted. Of late its use has become quite rare, and many new places with all the varieties have not a plant of this old favorite. Its habit of sucking is against it; but mingled with low-growing evergreens, its smooth greenish wood, twig-like branches, and lanceolate serrated leaves, in connection with the profusion of rose-shaped yellow flowers that it bears from March to July, make it very attractive and desirable. There is a small growing, variegated-leaved sort that suits well the foreground of a mass or group.

The KOELREUTERIA.—For the foreground of groups in which the Austrian or Scotch pines are prominent, the Koelreuteria paniculata, although only occasionally used, is really a very desirable plant. It is also well suited to a place in small gardens or lawns, and particularly where an erect, small, upright tree is wanted. Its stems are rather stiff than graceful, its leaves coarsely toothed and prominent; but its flowers borne at the ends of the shoots in long racemose spikes or panicles of a bright yellow color, give to the plant or tree a very fine appearance. The flowers are followed by large bladdery capsules, containing seeds, and in autumn the foliage before falling changes to a deep yellow. It succeeds in any good garden soil and makes a tree of about fifteen to twenty feet high.

The LABURNUM—*Cytisus.*—As a low growing ornamental tree or large shrub, the laburnum or golden chain has few rivals. The shape of the head is often irregular and picturesque; its foliage is of a smooth shining and beautiful green; it will grow in almost any soil, not wet, and when it flowers in June, its long pendant racemes of yellow or purple blooms make it extremely attractive and beautiful. The variety with yellow flowers, most commonly grown in the nurseries, makes a tree sometimes of fifteen to twenty feet in height; but it often loses its main stem, and sending up a cluster of stems, forms rather a shrub than a tree. The purple-flowering variety resembles in growth the common English, and occasionally its flowers revert back to the original yellow. There are several other varieties, but mainly differing only in form of foliage or period of bloom. They may be easily engrafted one upon the other, and thus one tree made to exhibit varied foliage and blooms, giving to it a unique appearance. As a single tree on small lawns, or for planting in cemeteries, or foregrounds of groups of trees, the laburnum is one of the most desirable.

The LILAC—*Syringa.*—The common lilac—*syringa vulgaris*—is well known all over the country; and although it has a great tendency to sucker, a little attention from year to year will enable the grower to keep it to a single stem, and it is then a beautiful tree in leaf, and pre-eminently so when in flower. Grouped with the snow-ball, red-bud, and other small-sized trees or large shrubs, it makes always an attractive appearance, and should not be thrown one side because it is common. There are several varieties with different shades of lilac and some pure white, and some with double flowers; all, however, of general habit in growth.

There is one known as Josikœa and one as Charles the Tenth, which have much the same habit of the old variety, but with more glossy leaves, and the former flowers of a deep purple, and the latter a reddish purple. There is also a variegated-leaved variety of the common *vulgaris.*

There is also a class of lilacs under the names of Chinese and Persian. The former, Chinese, is intermediate between *vulgaris* and *persica* in its habit of upright growth and with partially strong wood, while the latter has slender wood, sometimes almost recurved. There are a great many varieties, differing mainly in the shade of color in flower, while some are pure white. All of the lilacs are perfectly hardy; may be clipped and kept at any low height, and masses formed from a complete collection of the colors become very effective, especially if a little attention is paid, when planting, to arranging them with regard to the shades of the flowers and foliage. The cut-leaved lilac—*lasciniata*—is a pretty variety for the foreground of a mass or for a single point plant, on account of its curiously serrated or clipped leaves.

The MEZEREUM—*Daphne.*—The Daphne mezereum is a small shrub of about two to three feet in height, producing on its stems a profusion of pink or white flowers, according to the variety, in March or early April, before almost anything else. The flowers are very fragrant, and the plant on account of its period of blooming an exceedingly valuable one to plant. It needs a dry soil, deep and rich. The seeds or berries following the flowers become ripe and red in August or September, and are poisonous.

The MAGNOLIA.—Under the head of TREES we have named most of the varieties of magnolia in cultivation, because most of them form trees rather than shrubs; but the magnolia *purpurea* rarely, if ever, grows above six feet in height, and from its hardiness, broad, large, dark green foliage and numerous large cup-shaped purple and white flowers, demand for it a place in every garden, no matter how limited. As a single plant it is always attractive, and for massing with low-growing evergreens like the rhododendrons and kalmias, it is extremely valuable. There are two or three varieties, but not in general cultivation; the *gracilis* is probably the best; it has leaves narrower than the *purpurea*, and the petals of the flower are longer, and when opened fold back slightly.

Obovata pumila is a dwarf variety, forming only a little bush one and a half to two feet high, valuable for foregrounds of

FIG. 53.—MAGNOLIA PURPUREA.

shrubs; it, however, does not flower freely, and where only one or two plants are wanted, *purpurea* and *gracilis* should be selected.

The OLEASTER—*Elæagnus.*—The oleaster or wild olive tree is a shrub growing from eight to fifteen feet in height, and from its peculiar whitish foliage desirable for planting when it is wished to attract the eye to a particular point. For small grounds or positions where it comes directly under the eye, it has no claims to a place. The flowers are a pale yellow, fragrant in some varieties, but not prominent in beauty or attractiveness.

The FLOWERING PLUM—*Prunus.*—Under the name of *prunus trilobata* a new dwarf shrub has been recently introduced that promises great beauty, from its bearing a profusion of delicate pink semi-double flowers of about one inch in diameter thickly spread upon its long and slender branches. It is yet rare, but will doubtless soon find a place in every garden, where it should have a conspicuous position. It is quite hardy.

FIG. 54.—DOUBLE-FLOWERING PLUM.

The DOUBLE-FLOWERING PLUM—*Prunus.*—The double-flowering plum, or as often called sloe plum, is one of the finest small trees or large shrubs in the whole list. It is perfectly hardy; forms a round, compact head, and when in bloom its mass of little white double daisy-like flowers makes it a most attractive and beautiful object. Our engraving was copied from a plant we set in 1853. It should have a place by itself, open, upon the lawn.

The PRIVET or PRIM—*Ligustrum.*—The privet or prim is well known, as it is native to many sections. There are quite a large number of varieties, distinguished by their foliage. All are hardy, and their white flowers in spring and black berries in August make them beautiful although common. As hedge plants for ornamental purposes they are among the very best,

FIG. 55.—PURPLE FRINGE TREE.

growing freely in almost any soil, and keeping their foliage so late as to be almost sub-evergreen. We have seen clumps of the varieties in circles and clipped to give a round-headed mass of from fifteen to twenty feet diameter and six feet high in center, that were very attractive. Banks for screening low but unsightly objects may be formed readily by planting and shearing privet plants.

The PURPLE FRINGE TREE—*Rhus.*—The Venetian sumach or
purple fringe tree—*rhus cotinus*—is a much admired shrub from
its flowers, which are borne in large panicles, often proving
abortive, and their pedicles lengthening and becoming hairy
cover almost the entire tree. It sometimes is known as smoke
tree. It forms a small tree of ten to twelve feet high, suited for
a position by itself on a lawn, or better as a background plant
for a shrub group. Light dry soils suit it best. There are
several other varieties of rhus, many of them very ornamental

FIG. 56.—JAPAN QUINCE.

and worthy a place in large collections, but not so of positions
where they come under close observation. Rhus *veneneta* and
toxicodendron are extremely poisonous.

The JAPAN QUINCE—*Pyrus.*—The scarlet-flowering quince—
pyrus Japonica—is so well known that it seems hardly requisite
to do more than name it; and yet, well known as it is, its real
value as a shrub plant has been but little appreciated. Massed
with low-growing evergreens, or in clusters by itself upon the
lawn or border, its brilliancy of bloom always calls attention and

admiration, and in such positions it has been generally grown. As a hedge plant, in impenetrability it is second only to thorn or osage orange, while for beauty its blooms and foliage surpass all other plants. As a narrow low screen, it may be trained upright on wires, its side branches spurred in and made to present a perfect barrier, yet occupying only a very narrow space in width. There are now a number of varieties, varying in the color of their flowers from a delicate blush white to a

FIG. 57.—RED BUD.

deep rich crimson, and one with flowers semi or nearly double; and where only one plant is wanted, it is perhaps the best.

The RED BUD—*Cercis.*—The Judas tree, or, as more commonly known, the red bud—*cercis Canadensis*—forms a low, round-headed tree of from eight to fifteen feet in height, with round heart-shaped leaves of a dark bluish green above and a light sea green underneath, that make it remarkable as well as beautiful. It combines in planting harmoniously with the laburnum, snow-ball, thorn, and others, but its best position is just against or intermixed on the outskirts of a group of Austrian or Norway pines. There its profusion of bright pinkish red flowers, early in April and before the leaves have grown, borne all along on its branches, and often even on the main stem, are brought out so finely against the green of the pines, that it becomes one of the most pleasing and prominent of ornamental trees. There are two species in culti-vation, the American, *C. Canadensis*, and the European, *C.*

Fig. 58.—STUARTIA.

siliquastrum. The European blooms rather more freely than the American, and of a shade deeper in color. Any well-drained soil suits it.

The SNOW BERRY—*Symphoricarpus.*—The snow berry or St. Peter's wort is a common well-known old shrub, considered troublesome, when planted by itself or near borders, on account of its numerous suckers. It is a good shrub to use in rock-work, and its white fruit contrasts prettily when it is planted among low-growing shrub evergreens of narrow foliage. The varieties *racemosus* and *montanus* have white fruit, while the *vulgaris*, which is sometimes called Indian currant, has red fruit.

The STUARTIA.—The Stuartia *pentagynia* and *Virginica* are shrubs, natives of the higher portions of Virginia and Tennessee, and but little cultivated. They are partially hardy, fully so in sheltered positions, but not perfectly in open, clear exposures.

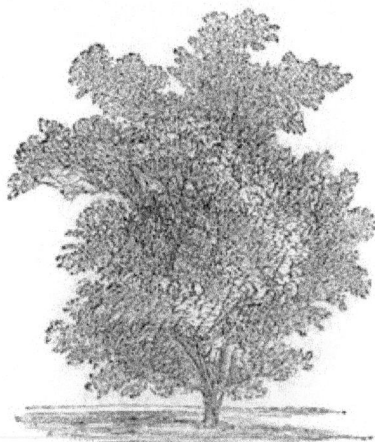

FIG. 59.—STRAWBERRY TREE.

The foliage is large, broad oval or ovate, and the flowers also large and pure white or with a shade of purple at the bottom of the petals, and the bloom is kept up some six weeks in succession in July and August. They are beautiful shrubs, and deserve a place and care in all gardens. Moist sandy loam containing considerable of vegetable mold suits their wants best.

The STRAWBERRY TREE—*Euonymus.*—The *euonymus Ameri-*

canus is known in various places under the different names of
strawberry tree, spindle tree, burning bush, etc., etc., and
although common is a much prized and very ornamental shrub
tree. The varieties are all good and desirable, as decorative
plants especially, when they can be used in connection with low-
growing evergreens, that assist in bringing more prominently
forward their bright rose-colored, crimson, or white fruit, which
generally hangs on all winter. The difference in the American
or European varieties, so far as ornamental use is regarded, is

Fig. 60.—Spiræa Prunifolia Flore Pleno.

mainly in the stronger growth of the European, it sometimes
making a tree of fifteen to twenty feet high, while the American
rarely grows over eight to twelve feet. The broad-leaved
variety, *latifolia*, is the handsomest in its foliage, and should be
used when only one plant is wanted.

The Spanish Broom—*Cytisus.*—The *Cytisus* var. *capitatus*,
hirsutus, and others, are small slender-growing plants, more
singular than handsome. They are not perfectly hardy, often

dying out after a few years' culture. Their value is mainly in some position near the top of some rocky point. Stems greenish yellow, flowers yellow in June and July.

The SOPHORA.—The *sophora Japonica* or Japan sophora is a beautiful round-headed tree, with smooth dark green bark and delicate blue green foliage. In the Northern and Middle States it is not perfectly hardy, but south of Philadelphia it stands pretty well, and deserves a place in all grounds where the climate will admit. It is sometimes grown in sheltered situa-

FIG. 61.—SPIRÆA CALLOSA.

tions at the North, amid evergreens or on poor thin soils, which seem to increase its hardiness, probably because of less succulence in the shoots and their better ripening.

The SPIRÆA.—The species and varieties of spiræa number over fifty, all of which are hardy and beautiful both in flower and foliage. A group may be formed alone of the varieties of spiræa that will give almost a continuation of flowers from May until October. Their growth is usually from two to four feet, coming from the crown by a number of stems in the natural way; but they may be kept to a single stem if desired, and clipped to any wished height. No place can be complete without many plants of the spiræa, and no garden is too small to admit of their introduction.

The following are among the most beautiful, viz., *prunifolia flore pleno, niconderti, thalictroides, crenata, lanceolata flore pleno, callosa alba*, and *floribunda*, all with white flowers. The

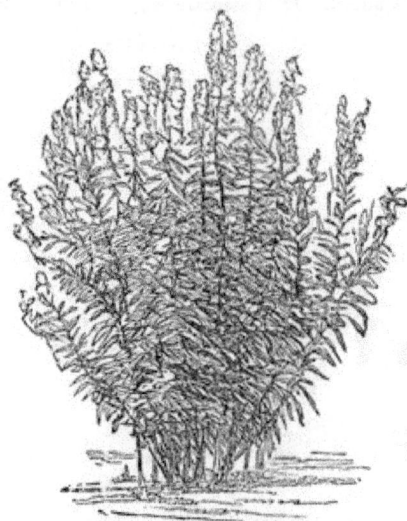

Fig. 62.—Spiræa Douglassi.

bella, Nobleana, eximia, callosa, Douglassii, and *Billardii* all have pink or rosy flowers. For decorating small lots in cemeteries all the spiræas are extremely well suited, especially those with white flowers.

The Snow-Ball—*Viburnum*.—The snow-ball or Guelder rose —*viburnum opulus*—is a well-known shrub, common in almost all gardens, and is truly one of the most ornamental shrubs or low trees known. It is suited either to mass with other deciduous plants or for grouping with low evergreens, or as a single plant. Its large clusters of white flowers early in May, and large, broad foliage, which toward autumn changes to a bright red, make it always handsome. There is a double-flowering variety, and several with variously shaped foliage; the lantana-leaved—

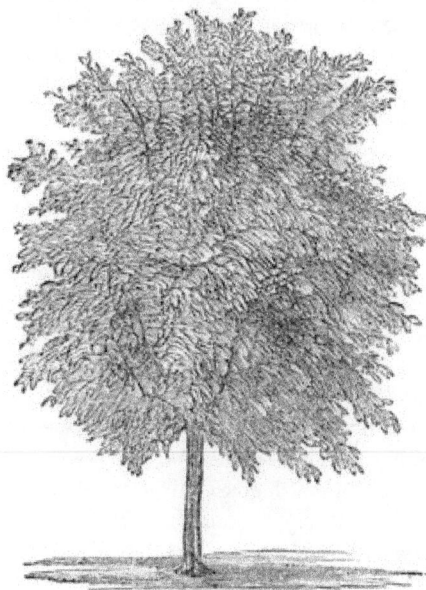

FIG. 63.—SILVER BELL.

lantanoides—being the best. The high bush cranberry—*viburnum oxycoccus*—is less ornamental in its flowers, but is more so in its fruit; and besides, it may be made to serve economically in the use of the fruit as a substitute for cranberries, while it fills a prominent place for ornament in the shrubbery. All of the varieties grow freely in any good garden soil.

The SNOW-DROP TREE—*Halesia.*—When in flower, the snow-drop or silver-bell tree is one of the most beautiful objects among shrub trees. The *tetraptera* or four-winged halesia produces a profusion of pure white flowers, like snow-drops, hanging in small clusters of four to eight all along its branches, that open during the last of April or early in May, before the leaves have grown, giving to the tree a most unique and beautiful effect from its waving, drooping mass of snowy white laced with the lines of dark brown from its branches. It makes a tree in height from fifteen to twenty feet.

The *diptera* or two-winged halesia does not bloom as early as the four-winged, but its flowers are larger and even more pure white, so that when in bloom the tree excites the admiration of all beholders. The foliage is larger and broader than the tetraptera, and altogether it is a variety that should be planted in all collections of any extent. As small lawn trees, or for prominent positions in small yards, both varieties are worthy a place, and when planted in front of a cluster of evergreens their beauty is much increased in effect.

The SWEET-SCENTED SHRUB — *Calycanthus.* — The sweet-scented shrub or allspice—*calycanthus floridus*—is a low shrub with broad, dark brownish green foliage and dark brown wood, producing a dull, dusky, chocolate-colored flower highly per-fumed, as is also the foliage, but less strong; and it is from this peculiar and agreeable perfume that the plant obtains universal favor and introduction into even the smallest gardens. Its growth is usually three to four feet high and as many broad, blossoms mostly produced in June, although, in some seasons, occasional flowers are produced until autumn. There are quite a number of varieties, varying in the form of foliage; and where room can be had for a cluster, their introduction by increased variety adds much to the beauty of a garden. The variety *floridus* is, however, the most fragrant and desirable when only one plant is wanted. Pieces of the root have a strong camphor scent. Rich, deep sandy, loamy soil, and a position partially shaded, produce the most healthy and vigorous growth.

The SYRINGA—*Philadelphus.*—The syringa or mock orange is another old and well-known shrub, some of its varieties being cultivated in nearly every garden in the United States. All are hardy, and grow freely in almost any soil or situation; all produce white flowers, many of them very fragrant, and some as beautiful as orange blossoms. The height attained by most varieties is from eight to ten feet, with stiff, erect stems and side branches that when in flower droop at the ends. There are two or three dwarf varieties, growing three to four feet, as *hirsutus, nana,* and others; but they do not flower as freely as the taller growing sorts, and are not desirable, because the Deutzias, spiræas, etc., may take their place. The syringas incline to throw up a cluster of stems; and if left and clipped at top may be formed into handsome shapes, or they may be kept to one single stem by cutting away all suckers. Of the varieties the Garland—*coronarius*—profuse flowered, *floribundus,* and Gordon's *Gordoniana* are among the best.

The TAMARISK—*Tamarix.*—The tamarisk is one of the most delicate and airy-like in appearance among shrubs. Its annual stems are long and slender, with very narrow juniper or red cedar-like foliage; and early in May the African and Algiers are covered all along the branches with small, bright pinkish red flowers, making them very attractive and especially beautiful when seen from among a group of junipers, savins, etc. There are several other varieties, as the German, French, etc., all more or less tender except in sheltered situations or having winter protection, when grown in the Northern and Middle States.

The plant should be clipped back occasionally, otherwise it is liable to grow too rambling, irregular, and tall, and its beauty and quantity of bloom become reduced. Any good loamy soil suits it.

The WEIGELA.—Among all the plants introduced during the past thirty years, we do not think any one more truly beautiful

FIG. 64.—WHITE FRINGE TREE.

than the *Weigela rosea* when in flower. It is a shrub of the easiest cultivation, growing freely in almost any soil, forming a round regular bush; and when loaded with its large clusters of rose-colored flowers, borne upon the side branches and at the extremities of the shoots, it has a slightly drooping and graceful form, extremely beautiful. Since its introduction varieties have been produced, all very beautiful, but none surpassing the *rosea*. The *amabilis* has a somewhat larger foliage, and a habit of sometimes blooming in autumn, which makes it quite desirable. *Alba* has flowers almost white or of a delicate pinkish white, and *Desbois* has flowers like rosea, except they are darker when first opened. The variegated-leaved weigela is a strong grower, and desirable on account of its foliage, being edged with yellow.

The plants may be grown in clusters or to a single stem. In the latter way the side branches become horizontal, almost drooping, especially when in flower, and for single specimens present in this manner perhaps the best and most pleasing effect.

The WHITE FRINGE TREE—*Chionanthus.*—The white fringe tree or Virginian snow-flower—*chionanthus Virginica*—is a shrub or low tree with dark green foliage and producing a profusion of drooping racemes of pretty white flowers in the month of June. It delights in moist soil, and by the side of water grows vigorously, and is, when in flower, an extremely pretty shrub. In dry soils its growth is very slow, and it is not specially desirable as compared with many other plants that grow freely and bloom at the same period.

G

INDEX.

DECIDUOUS TREES.

WEEPING DECIDUOUS TREES.

EVERGREEN TREES.

WEEPING EVERGREEN TREES.

EVERGREEN SHRUBS.

ORNAMENTAL DECIDUOUS SHRUBS.